# GEORGIA ON MY MIND

# GEORGIA ON MY MIND

*The Nat Gonella Story*

## Ron Brown
in conjunction with
## Cyril Brown

MILESTONE PUBLICATIONS

Published by Milestone Publications
62 Murray Road, Horndean
Portsmouth, Hants. PO8 9JL

Design Brian Iles

Typeset by Inforum Ltd, Portsmouth

Printed and bound in Great Britain by
R. J. Acford, Industrial Estate, Chichester, Sussex

British Library Cataloguing in Publication Data

Brown, Ron, *1932-*
    Georgia on my mind : the Nat Gonella story.
    1.  Gonella, Nat      2.  Jazz musicians—Great
Britain—Biography
    I.  Title      II.  Brown, Cyril
    788'.1'0924        ML419.G6

ISBN 0-903852-68-3

# Acknowledgements

The authors are indebted to several people for their help and encouragement whilst compiling the information for this biography, we would especially like to thank Digby Fairweather, Beryl Bryden, Hugh Palmer, Bill Reed, Pat and Tony Wing, Patrick Griffiths, Dorothy Gonella, Norman Facy, Doug and Dorry Whitfield, and Chris Hayes. Formerly with the *Melody Maker* for many years, Chris is indeed a veritable mine of information. We also count ourselves as being fortunate to have the subject of the book, Nat Gonella, on hand to confirm and very often expand on the facts and stories that grace the pages.

For additional sources of information we were grateful for the use of extracts from the following: *Popular Music Weekly* 1924–1938, *Rhythm Magazine* 1936–1939, *Who's Who In Variety* 1946, *Daily Mail, Daily Sketch, Evening News, Daily News* (New South Wales), *Evening Standard, Radio Pictorial* 1936–1939, a large selection of record catalogues, and *Modern Style Trumpet Playing* by Nat Gonella 1935.

Most of the photographs in this book come from Nat Gonella's own collection and from the authors' collections. Acknowledgement for other photographs has been indicated in the captions where the source is known, however, should there be any omissions in this respect, the publishers will gladly add any appropriate acknowledgements to future editions.

# Contents

# Foreword

Perhaps, as Whitney Balliett once wrote, nostalgia is cheap witch-craft. But, Nat Gonella and his Georgians will always begin with a memory for me: of sitting on the deep green inlaid arm of my father's comfortable armchair, glancing through sunshot windows to waving green fields, and scanning his old E.M.I. catalogues for jazz entries. The feeling was exciting and one degree furtive – akin to thumbing through his *Lilliput* magazines in search of their one haughty pin-up. The E.M.I. catalogue was equally sparing with its jazz délices, but one name appeared with reliable frequency: Nat Gonella.

The name on its own was jazzy enough. A lucky combination of happy accidents (christian name Nathaniel, surname an Italian inheritance) — somehow ensured that he was already a great jazzman. "The Georgians" sounded exactly right too, and so did the tunes they played; jazz standards, swing songs of the day, and intriguing novelties that cross-fertilized the jazz aesthetic with an injection of music hall, well within the sounds of Bow Bells and Billy Cotton. It was a heady brew, but hard to track down; no records in the cupboard or at the local shop. So, Bing Crosby and Louis Armstrong continued their carillon uninterrupted in our old country house. The name of Nat Gonella was, just for now, an intriguing echo in the spring breeze.

For a schoolboy long on enthusiasm, but short on pocket money, the best way to buy records was from the local junkshop, run by Harry Strauss, a patient saint of a man. Day after day, Harry put up with my determined re-searching of the same pile of old 78s. I found lots of Harry James and Artie Shaw, plenty of Sid Phillips, Humphrey Lyttelton and Freddy Randall, and occasionally a Joe Daniels or a Louis Armstrong, but never a Nat Gonella. I was more intrigued. But the reason came to me at last via Mr. and Mrs. Bones of Hackney — the apocryphal couple who control popular trends in the music industry. They had seen him at their music hall, jitter-bugged to his records, and made love to his romantic songs. And while jazz fans sometimes sell their records, Mr. and Mrs. Bones very seldom sell their memories.

Many years passed before I found an original Gonella record. There it was, at the bottom of a pile of once-loved old records in an antique shop: a maroon-labelled, gold-lettered revelation that proclaimed: "Don't Cross Your Fingers, Cross Your Heart" sung and played by Nat Gonella, backed with "Stop Beating Around The Mulberry Bush. I hurried home to make my first discoveries.

The loudspeaker revealed a warm rhythmic singer bouncing through a boldly-intervalled swing tune of the type that became the Second World War's first casualty. A trumpet of gold tone, assured command and able swing, through which an English promise ran, as old and bold as John Bull himself. A picture of Nat Gonella, jazz trumpeter, began to emerge. More detail was added when Nobby Brand, an old friend and Gonella fan, presented me with a cassette of vintage Georgians. I listened intently and quickly observed that the trumpeted Gonella-Armstrong resemblance was much overplayed. The Georgia boy's warm, intense, highly-correct trumpet playing, with its curt tonguing and studious vibrato, rang a bell for Kneller Hall – twenty miles west from his Islington home – as well as New Orleans. The result was a compelling swing trumpeter, without the simple perfection that made Armstrong a genius, but with a facility and direct lyricism that found an echo in players such as Mouse Randolph, Dick Clark and Wingy Manone. Nat Gonella sounded like such men, but historically he was their peer, and greater than most. It may have been that Louis would have run him off the stage had they met in some fantasy-world trumpet cutting contest, but Jabbo Smith, Jack Purves, George Mitchell or Herman Autry would have been out in the street before Nat.

So, where, if anywhere, were the similarities with Louis? Certainly they existed, in some of the technical facility to begin with. Like Louis, Nat was a very good trumpeter, as easily able to lead the Roy Fox brass section as to play creative jazz. He had the confidence of a natural leader; confidence enough to transfer his in-flight imagination unflawed to records, and on occasion to play for Louis himself. He had the strength of character, akin to Louis, to let his trumpet-playing survive all the rigours and pressures of showbusiness and stardom. And like Louis, he also had the physical, and mental, strength and discipline to play to the top of his range every night, without allowing his art to be dulled by beautiful girls, late nights, or wondering if he would make the top E at the close of "Basin Street Blues".

To experience his pure joy of playing, listen to the 1934 recording that Nat made with Brian Lawrence: "Sweet Sue, Just You". There's that broad-as-a-mile British sound, and the confident inspiration that slowly and naturally brings the performance to a climax, plus the effortless movement between registers, copybook accuracy and easy ability in top registers. Above all, the technical *joie de vivre* that transmits itself to a performance when a trumpet player knows that he is playing well is much in evidence. If a distinction has to be made, for Louis Armstrong, the *joie de vivre* made itself apparent in the top one hundred elemental top C's of "Shine." For Nat Gonella it was the cheeky "watch-me-now" triple tongued runs of "Sweet Sue, Just You" that anticipated Charlie Shavers by a good five years, and were created – like the small genius he was – by Nat himself from a jazz vacuum. One thing is clear, Armstrong and Gonella together were young men exulting in their command over that physically challenging – and rewarding – adversary, the trumpet. And jazz was all the richer for it.

Progressing through the dance music and jazz scene of the 1930s, Nat's style broadened with the music trends of the war years. Listen to the New Georgians in "Song Of Songs" – without losing its identity, the trumpet sound has moved with the times. An on-form Harry James would have played no better than Nat Gonella on this record. It was only with the advent of bebop that our subject, for once, stopped short. His reaction to the highly self-conscious innovation of bop was simple, and after a short flirtation, final. "Gas oven music" he called it, and, agree or not, his three-word analysis carried the same conviction as something else once said by Louis Armstrong, jazz's most perceptive philosopher. "Man you don't pose, never," said Armstrong, and while bebop was never truly a pose – for Britain's first classic jazz trumpeter, now approaching forty, it really had to be.

Over the following years, Nat's fortunes fluctuated considerably; a return to the music hall, playing in small clubs and pubs, and on occasion, nowhere. Where he had once earned thousands, he was glad to take home a few pounds in order to survive. But, as always, there was that friendly Cockney voice that tried to persuade you that "it was really all a bit of a lark", nothing more. "Just a bit of a lark" is the way that Nat Gonella would have you remember his life but, for me, the Nat Gonella story – supreme success story though it is – is also a grand example of fate at her most ungenerous. At least three luckless "invasions", Poland in 1939, modern jazz in 1946, and Liverpool in 1962, dealt hammer blows to a career that should have achieved immortality by the time he was fifty.

But his life – up, down, and all ways – impinged on our lives too. The vision you carry with you depends on when, for you, it happened first. It could have been when Nat Gonella emerged from behind some Moss Empire curtain in the Thirties to climb to an effortless top C. It could have been when, smiling and philosophical, he returned to the jazz scene with an all-star band in the early Sixties. Or maybe your vision is more recent, of the youthful impish man who steps on to the stage of Gosport Jazz Club in the 1980s to mug his way through "St. James Infirmary" for a crowd of delighted patrons. My own vision is a composite, drawn from a picture painted in words by friend Tiny Winters. In this vision a young swing trumpeter in a check jacket walks jauntily out of a smoky Bag o' Nails Club into the chirruping morning air of a Mayfair dawn. His trumpet is under his arm, and all the world is at his feet.

Ladies and Gentlemen, we present the last king, the first legend of British jazz . . . Nat Gonella and his story. Ring up the happy curtain!

*[signature: Digby Fairweather]*

1985

*Nat Gonella, Britain's hottest trumpeter, in 1934.*

# 1

**OPENING BARS.**

The errand-boy walked jauntily along the street, his arms clutching a large cardboard box, and his lips whistling a popular song of the day, "Yes, We Have No Bananas". About him roared the traffic sounds associated with the London of the 1920s, delivery vans, taxi-cabs, and the double-decker bus. He was halfway along Union Street when suddenly he stopped in his tracks, his eyes drawn to the window of a music shop. The sign above the window read: "Rudd & Company. Manufacturers and Importers of Pianofortes & Harmoniums". However, it was not the sign that had brought him to a halt, the object of his attention was a shiny cornet that stood out from the rest of the instruments on display. The cornet was second-hand, but it was in a reasonable condition.

The lad stood gazing at the instrument for some time, eventually breaking the spell to inspect the accompanying price-tag. Phew, £3. 10s, a fortune indeed, when he was earning only eighteen shillings a week, a good portion of which he had to hand over to his mother. Heaving a sigh, he gave the cornet one last longing look, then hurried away to deliver the parcel.

His working day over, the boy returned to the family home in Holloway, north London, where his widowed mother struggled to make ends meet. He had no intention of saying anything about the cornet but, as the evening progressed, his mind kept straying to the instrument, and he found that he was unable to contain himself any longer. When he had finished relating the highlight of his day to his mother, to his surprise, instead of ridiculing his desire to possess the instrument, she was sympathetic. She could tell that he was serious, so she suggested that he should go back to the store and approach the dealer about purchasing the cornet on easy terms.

The following day, the errand-boy took the first opportunity he had to return to the music shop. Summoning his courage, he stepped inside to take a closer look at the cornet. From behind his counter, the dealer watched the boy intently. He was amused but at the same time intrigued that an errand-boy should be so interested in an instrument that had a price-tag of £3. 10s.

A few moments passed, then the dealer rose from his stool, crossed to the window, and lifted out the cornet. He offered it to the lad, more or less daring him to play it. The youngster placed the horn on his lips then, to the amazement of the dealer, he proceeded to give a faultless rendition of "Yes, We Have No Bananas". His one-man audience was obviously impressed, and realized that the boy was not wasting his valuable time. The bargaining began, culminating in an agreement that if the boy put down a deposit of five shillings, he could pay off the balance at half-a-crown a week. As he stepped out of the shop into Union Street, the boy held the cornet as if it were made of glass.

In the weeks that followed, the Holloway neighbourhood in which he lived resounded to the sound of that cornet being blown in practice. Those who clamped their hands to their ears could hardly have realized then that within ten years they would be only too happy to pay money to hear the same person play. The purchase of that cornet in 1923 proved to be an important turning point in the life of that young man – Nat Gonella.

The story of Nat Gonella is essentially about a chirpy Cockney kid who overcame considerable adversity in his early years, including poor health and an orphanage upbringing, to become a legend in the world of showbusiness, enjoying the patronage of royalty, the friendship of some of the stars, and the adulation of millions. He emerged from the infant years of radio and talking pictures to make his mark in several facets of entertainment, notably dance music, the variety stage, and jazz.

The world of dance music, with its immaculately attired ladies and gentlemen in plush nightclubs, occupied in sipping champagne or gyrating their bodies to the sound of bands led by such revered names as Roy Fox, Ambrose, Lew Stone, and Billy Cotton; the variety theatres, allowing the masses to see their radio and gramophone idols in the flesh, Gracie Fields, George Formby, Al Bowlly, Max Miller and Max Wall, to name a few; finally, the world of jazz, with those such as Louis Armstrong, Fats Waller, Benny Carter, Wingy Manone, Bobby Hackett, Benny Goodman, Tommy Dorsey, Harry James, and Britain's Humphrey Lyttelton. Nat Gonella knew and performed with all of them, and many more.

Although he has been mentioned in several star biographies over the years, Nat's own story has never been committed to book form, apart from the occasional feature in a newspaper or magazine. It is true that television and radio programmes have been devoted to him, "This Is Your Life" in 1960 and "Omnibus" in the late Seventies, plus a regular mention on Alan Dell's "Dance Band Days" on Radio 2, but how can the life of such a musical phenomenon as Nat Gonella be given justice in a mere thirty minutes? In the following pages we will attempt to rectify this by giving an insight into Gonella the Man, as well as Gonella the Musician. Although he made and lost a fortune, climbed to the top of his chosen profession, and slipped to the bottom, he is not a bitter man. It is uncommon to hear him speak ill of anyone but, in a rare criticism relating to his musical contemporaries of yesteryear, he once said: "The trouble with some of the old-time band leaders was that they thought they were Jesus Christ, and that the money and the applause would last forever. That is something that you cannot be certain of in showbusiness; the musical tastes of the paying public change like the wind, as I know only too well." Being big-headed is something that Nat himself could not be accused of for he has always kept his feet firmly on the ground and has never exercised the "I am a Star" routine.

Having survived sixty years in the music business, Nat has somehow managed to retain his perpetual Cockney cheerfulness and wit. He has taken life as it came, his philosophy may be described as "whatever will be, will be". In fact, "No Regrets" could also be deemed as a suitable title for this biography, however, on reflection there is really only one title that a book concerning the life of Nat Gonella could be called "Georgia On My Mind" for this song and the name of the man are synonymous.

So, let us return to the London of yesteryear and recall the events that preceded the purchase of that cornet in 1923, and subsequently the fluctuating fortunes that followed for the purchaser.

# 2

**THE BOYHOOD YEARS.**

There are very few people with showbusiness aspirations who are fortunate enough to be blessed with a name that looks good on a film poster or a theatre bill, which may explain how someone can start life as Albert Hardcastle, and finish it as Rocky Stardust. The subject of this book had no such problems, he was born Nat Gonella, a name that is immediately memorable and outstanding enough to grace any form of publicity.

Although they had lived in Great Britain for several generations, as the name would suggest, the Gonella family is of Italian origin. For a showbiz connection we can go back to the 15th Century where an Italian nobleman, Nicolo d'Este, had a jester named Gonella in his court.

For the next Gonella entertainment association we must move forward some four hundred years or so to London in the latter half of the last century, where Joseph Gonella made his living by playing the banjo. He was described officially as a street minstrel, which one may suppose is a polite term for busker. However, evidence does suggest that he also played in a black-face minstrel troupe from time to time. Joseph married a young lady named Emma Cobb, they made their home in Prospect Terrace, St. Pancras, and proceeded to provide another generation of Gonellas.

The particular offspring from this union that concerns our story is Richard Henry Gonella, who was born on 24 May, 1871. When he was old enough to commence his working life, Richard did not choose to follow his father into the entertainment business, he worked with horses, gradually progressing to a position as a horse-cab driver.

Richard took a shine to a girl named Elizabeth Susan Finnes who also had connections in the transport business via her father, Nathaniel Finnes, who was a carman. Their romance blossomed, and subsequently Elizabeth became a Gonella on 6 June 1897, the wedding taking place at All Saints Church in the Battle Bridge area of Kings Cross. Nathaniel Finnes was on hand to give away his daughter, but Joseph Gonella had died by this time. Richard and Elizabeth set up home at 15, Edward Square, Islington, which was off the Caledonian Road. Over the following sixteen years they had seven children and life in those years could be described as: "They were poor, but they were happy."

Nathaniel was the Gonella's fourth child, arriving into the world on 7 March, 1908. The popular song of that year was "Oh, Oh, Antonio" but he was christened Nathaniel Charles Gonella after his grandfather. Nathaniel, whom we shall refer to as Nat, spent his early years in the rough and tough district of Kings Cross, an area he jokingly described later as "a place where the inhabitants eat their young".

His earliest memories are of playing in the streets with the other kids in the neighbourhood, getting up to the usual childhood pranks such as banging door-knockers and jumping on and off the backs of delivery carts. Without the modern diversion of television, the entertainment in those days was very much in the streets. The Caledonian Road had plenty to offer, in addition to the mass of small shops and street stalls that adorned this road in the early part of this century, the Caledonian Cattle Market and the Agricultural Hall were not far away, and, of course, there was always the stirring sight of magnificent steam trains puffing in and out of Kings Cross Station.

As a cab driver, Richard Gonella did not exactly make a fortune but his family were quite adequately provided for, faring far better than many of the other London families in those years between the Boer War and World War I. When horseless carriages began to make their presence felt, Richard moved with the times and made the transition from a horse to a motorised cab. As the family expanded, they moved nearby to bigger and better living accommodation at 22, Edward Square.

But tragedy struck when Richard became ill and, despite the efforts of Dr Beardmore, he died from pulmonary tuberculosis on 27 September, 1915, aged 44.

The bottom had fallen out of the Gonella family's world. Without their chief provider, they were in dire straits. The eldest son was the only member of the family old enough to work, and his wages were but a few shillings a week. In those days the only help available for families in distress came from charitable institutions such as the Islington Board of Guardians, and it was this organization that came to the aid of the Gonella family. They approached Elizabeth with a view to taking all her children and placing them in homes where they would be cared for and taught trades but she could not bear the thought of being parted from them and resisted fiercely. Eventually, a compromise was struck. Much as it broke her heart, Elizabeth agreed that the three youngest children should go into a home. This trio comprised Nat, by now aged seven, his younger brother, Bruts, and their sister, Jessie. Bruts Gonella, born on 31 January 1911, had Nat to thank for his unusual first name rather than his parents. He was christened Adolphus James but as Adolphus was not the ideal sort of a name to use among tough orphanage kids, Nat called him Bruts, an abbreviation of brother, and it stuck.

St. Mary's Guardians School was designated as home for Nat, Bruts and Jessie for the remainder of their childhood years. Situated in Hornsey Road, north London, it had previously served as the Islington Workhouse School. As they were taken through the entrance gates for the first time, removed from the care of a loving mother and that special bond of kinship enjoyed by large families, it would not be difficult to understand the feelings of the three little mites. However, despite the grim exterior, St. Mary's was by no means a Dickensian type of institution and, under the guidance of the principal, George Johnson, it performed a valuable service in preparing the inmates for the hard world that they would encounter outside when they began their working lives.

Although there was a strong emphasis on discipline and the necessity to keep oneself clean and tidy, the inmates were well cared for, and Nat and his brother and sister probably fared better than the rest of their family who were roughing it back in Kings Cross. To the credit of the school, Nat always stressed that he was very fortunate to have spent most of his childhood there, and was convinced that his success in later life was largely due to his upbringing at St. Mary's.

Akin to pupils in other schools, the boys and girls had regular lessons and played the usual sports, in addition to which they were taught a trade. From his early days at the school Nat displayed an aptitude for carpentry, and indeed became quite proficient at using a hammer, saw, or chisel. The carpentry teacher was a rather elderly man, and although he was good at his trade, unfortunately he was very deaf. Despite this, he was very fond of music and always attended any concerts given by the school band.

Of the various sporting activities, football was Nat's first love, and secretly he nourished a dream that one day he would play professionally for his favourite team, Tottenham Hotspur, a club that he was to support all his life. In his early playing days, he showed more enthusiasm than skill but, eventually, he was good enough to earn a regular place in the school team. They may have been the victims of circumstance but the inmates of St. Mary's always held their heads high, with the young footballers taking on the role of ambassadors for the institution whenever they had to play against an outside team. If the rules of the game had allowed extra points for the smartest turnout, they would have topped the league every week. The team's shirts, socks and shorts were dealt with by the school laundry but members had to clean and grease their boots until they shone.

Another occasion when the boys and girls of St. Mary's were certain to be clean and smartly turned-out was on visiting day, which took place once a month. Elizabeth Gonella was always sure to be on time for the visits, very often bringing other members of the family with her. A weekly treat for the inmates was when they were marched to nearby Finsbury Park, a veritable green heaven, where they were allowed to run and play to their hearts' content.

Despite this slice of freedom, some of the children became

homesick from time to time, and on occasion attempted to escape from the confines of the building. Even Nat tried this once, with another lad named George Latimer. However, they did not get very far, their break for freedom finishing in a north London police station. The school was notified immediately and a master named Whitworth came to the station to collect the two wayward boys. The first thing that he made them do was to remove their braces, following which they were marched back to St. Mary's with their hands in their pockets in order to keep their trousers up. On their arrival back at the school, Nat and George were ordered to take their hands out of the pockets. This resulted in their trousers falling to the ground, thus exposing their backsides for the ensuing punishment.

The school had an excellent brass band that played a march every morning as the children assembled in the dining hall for breakfast, it was also in great demand to play at local fetes and garden parties. The highlight of the year was when the whole school was marched to a church for the harvest festival service, led by the school band in their resplendent uniforms of green with gold braid. In fact, it was the smart uniform that first attracted Nat's attention, any notion of actually playing an instrument was secondary. Band rehearsals were held every weekday evening, and anyone who felt that they would like the opportunity of learning to play a musical instrument was encouraged to apply for an interview with the teacher, Mr. Clarke. Late of Kneller Hall, William Clarke was an excellent musician, having formerly served as the Bandmaster of the 1st East Surrey Regiment.

In later years, Nat came to realize how fortunate he had been to have been taken under the wing of such a fine tutor. However, at this early stage, young Gonella was certainly no budding musical genius, and had his hopes severely shattered at his first interview to join the band. Mr. Clarke handed him a cornet, which the confident nine-year-old lad promptly put to his mouth to blow. Some moments passed, his cheeks changed several hues of red, and still the horn failed to emit one solitary note. The more annoyed and frustrated the boy got, the more amused Mr. Clarke became.

*St Mary's Guardians school band, 1917. Nat is sitting at the right of drum, holding cornet.* (Gonella Collection)

Eventually, the kindly old teacher relieved the lad of the cornet, patted him gently on the head, and advised him to come back when he was older.

Fortunately for the music world, Nat was not going to let the small fact that he could not play a note stop him from wearing one of those grand uniforms, and returned to Mr. Clarke the following week to politely inform him that he was now one week older. How could he reject such enthusiasm? Especially when it came from one with such angelic features. He suggested that the lad might begin by playing the drums. It did not really matter to Nat, as long as he could wear a uniform. And so, Nat Gonella's entrance into the world of music was secured by playing the drums, not the cornet.

After a few months he was fairly proficient at drumming, but all the while he felt a compelling urge to master the secrets of the cornet, and whenever he had the opportunity he would sneak into the bandroom for an unscheduled practice session. By experimenting with the mouthpiece he managed to produce the odd squeak or two, which to Nat was real progress. Unknown to him, Mr. Clarke had been keeping an eye and ear on his prowess, and consequently decided that the boy had an aptitude for music. The moment had come for him to initiate the youngster into the art of cornet playing.

The willing pupil and the patient tutor worked well together, and Nat's progress was indeed quite rapid. The first thing that he learnt was the orthodox non-pressure system, his teacher impressing on him the importance of blowing easily rather than too hard. This was advice that Nat was able to expand on and pass to aspiring players some years later in his book *Modern Style Trumpet Playing*. In his book, Nat recommends that the mouthpiece is placed at the centre of the mouth but he always played from the side. He developed this unusual style at school when he was troubled by cold sores and split lips, at their worst in the winter. His lips refused to heal so, through necessity, he used the side embrochure for blowing. It remained with him for the rest of his playing career. Mr. Clarke tried several times to get Nat to revert to blowing from the centre of the mouth but, in the end, he conceded that it suited Nat better. In later years, when he was an established trumpet star, many up-and-coming trumpeters emulated him by playing from the side of the mouth, which always amused Nat because, technically, it was wrong.

Members of the school band were taught to read music, their repertoire consisting largely of marches and light classical pieces. Although there was definitely no encouragement to play dance music, several members of St Mary's School band made this particular aspect of music their career in later life. Nat's pal, George Latimer, was a fine trombonist, and there were two brothers, Sid and Ernie Fearn, who later played in the trumpet section for Jack Payne and Billy Cotton respectively. Neither must we forget Nat's brother, Bruts, who was another of Mr. Clarke's star pupils, and, like Nat, was destined to make his mark in the music world. So, the school band had a wealth of young talent, and enjoyed a good measure of success in all the contests in which they took part, their biggest achievement being when they gained third place in the junior section of a national competition at the Crystal Palace. Naturally, Mr. Clarke was extremely proud of his boys that day.

By the time that Nat had reached the age of thirteen, his personal star was riding very high, in his own words: "I guess that I was something of a big-shot!" This was not really boasting for he was the school's Head Boy, captain of the football team, Sergeant of the school band, he was winning awards for his skill at carpentry, and, if that were not enough, he won the school boxing championship. Nat's version of his win in the final was that he happened to catch his opponent with a good blow on the nose, it would not stop bleeding, so he was given the verdict on a technical knockout. Just when everything was going so well for him, something happened to shatter his hopes and dreams, he contracted rheumatic fever and had to spend six months in the school hospital, at one stage hovering between life and death.

When he was fit enough to leave the hospital, the doctor warned him that the fever had left him with a seriously weakened heart, the outcome being that strenuous activities such as playing football or blowing the cornet were things of the past. This was devastating news for a youngster whose life revolved around sport and music. However, all was not lost, Mr. Clarke, who had taken such a shine to the little lad, came to his aid by suggesting that Nat might try an instrument that was less taxing on his heart. Anything was better than not playing at all, so he learnt to play the E-flat tenor horn and the violin. Such was his progress on the horn that within a few months of taking it up, he won a soloist's prize in the North London Band Contest.

As Nat approached the age of 15, the time was drawing near when he would have to leave St. Mary's in order to go out into the world and fend for himself. On leaving the school, many boys went straight into the Army, especially those who had played in the school band. World War I had ended only five years earlier, the peace celebration parades were still fresh in people's minds, their strong feelings of patriotism stirred by the sight of soldiers marching through the streets to the sound of a military band. Once again, it was the uniform that attracted the young Gonella, and he duly presented himself at the recruiting office in Westminster with a view to joining the 15th Hussars. Why not, he may have been only 5ft.3ins. tall and weighed nine stone ten pounds, but he was very tough and wiry. All went well until the medical examination, the Medical Officer was thorough and detected the weak heart, and subsequently informed Nat that the King's Army would have to try to struggle on without his services.

What was he to do? Even the prospect of entering the carpentry trade was closed to him, his tuition having ceased because of his delicate health following the fever. Then someone suggested tailoring. His time to leave was getting closer, so Nat was put on a crash course to learn the rudiments of this profession during his last months at the school. By the time he left he could make buttonholes, and had even managed to turn a pair of trousers. The employment department at the school worked hard to ensure that their young charges should get as good a start to their working lives as possible, a decent job being the top priority. After much searching, they secured a position for Nat in a London tailoring establishment.

The day arrived for the budding tailor to pass through the gates of St. Mary's for the last time, leaving behind him the building that had been his home for eight years, and the teachers he had come to respect. This institution was not destined to survive many more years after his departure and closed in the early 1930s. There was little cause to feel sorry for young Nathaniel Charles Gonella as he left the orphanage to commence his working life, the school had done a fine job in preparing him for the struggle ahead, instilling in him a strong measure of independence and self-preservation, and perhaps the most important factor of all, it had introduced him to the marvel of music.

# 3

**YOUNG MAN OF MUSIC.**

In conjunction with the Guardians School, a hostel existed in London where former inmates could stay after they had left. On receiving their pay packets at the end of the week, they immediately passed them over to the principal of the hostel who, after deducting money for food and board, would divide the remainder between the boy and his parents, or dependants as the case might be. The hostel was run on strict disciplinary lines, the boys had to be in bed by a certain time and church attendance was compulsory on Sundays.

When he first left school, 15-year-old Nat stayed at the hostel and it was from there that he set off for his first day of work at the tailoring shop, which was in Albany Street near Regents Park. He spent the first day stitching lapels, on the second day he stitched lapels, and again on the third day. Those three days were sufficient to convince him that he was not cut out to be a tailor so he handed in his needle and thread and collected six shillings for his efforts. Nat always maintained that he was not suited as a tailor because he could not sit cross-legged long enough!

His decision to leave the tailoring trade after three inglorious days was not well received at the hostel. But Nat soon found himself another job. He was strolling along Great Portland Street one day when a notice outside a furriers establishment caught his eye: WANTED, ERRAND-BOY. After entering the premises and stating his business, he was ushered to the proprietor's office for an interview, the outcome being that he was offered the position at a wage of fifteen shillings a week. Nat did not hesitate, he accepted and started work there almost immediately. Out of that fifteen shillings, the hostel retained ten shillings, his mother was allotted half-a-crown, and Nat had the remaining half-a-crown.

He was extremely happy with his new job, it allowed him to get out and about in London, and the boss treated him kindly. He also made friends with a charming French couple who worked at the furriers, and it was directly due to their encouragement that he got into the entertainment business.

Nat's duties as an errand-boy were not without their moments of drama. There was one particular incident that he would remember for the rest of his life. One day he was instructed to deliver a very expensive fur coat to a large store in Regent Street, opting to travel there by bus. He boarded the bus, and, as it was a hot day, he stowed his parcel in the baggage compartment under the stairs and went and sat on the top deck. It was indeed a lovely day, and he soon became engrossed in viewing the busy London traffic scene from his high perch. Suddenly, he realized that the bus had arrived at the stop he wanted, so he raced down the stairs and jumped off the platform just as the vehicle was moving away from the stop. As he paused on the pavement he had the feeling that there was something missing. Horror of horrors, he had left the fur coat on the bus.

With the thought flashing through his mind that on his weekly wage of fifteen shillings it would take him about thirty years to pay for the coat, he ran across Piccadilly Circus in a blind panic. A bus loomed in front of him but was it the one he had been riding on? He threw himself on to the platform and there was the parcel in the luggage section as he had left it. A very relieved errand-boy disembarked at the next stop.

With this near-catastrophe behind him, Nat began to settle in the job, and it was not long before he was awarded a rise that took his weekly wage to eighteen shillings. This helped him to make the momentous decision to leave the hostel and to live with his mother at home, the reasoning being that the extra money would considerably boost the family exchequer. At that time the Gonella family were living in George's Road, Holloway, a few streets away from the Caledonian Market. The road was in a typical 1920s working-class district, rows of terraced houses with front doors straight off the pavement, and interiors that were vastly overcrowded. Akin to countless other city streets of that period, George's Road was a fairly self-contained community, having the usual selection of small shops. The latter included Ernie Popple's bakers shop, Mr. Mansi's fruit and veg store, a sweetshop run by Ed Aimes, and Jim Ellis's hairdressing salon where Nat got his short-back-and-sides. The road also possessed no fewer than five public houses. George's Road is still on the street map in the 1980s, although much of it has been swallowed by a large council housing estate. There is still one pub left, originally the Royal Victory, the name was changed in 1982 to The Moynham Arms.

Nat had not been back in the family home long before he realized what marvellous value the boys got by living in the subsidized hostel; he was glad to be home among the family that he had been parted from for so long but it was a struggle financially. Still, Elizabeth Gonella had a little job, the rest of the family helped out as best they could, and somehow they survived.

And so to that momentous day, 29 November, 1923, when Nat became infatuated with that cornet in the window of the music shop in Union Street. After he had successfully negotiated for the purchase of the instrument, the hours could not pass quickly enough until he had it back home in the refuge of his bedroom. It was not until he raised the horn to his lips that he was reminded of the doctor's warning two years earlier. Certainly he had played it in the music shop without thinking but that had only been for a couple of minutes; would his heart stand up to the strain of playing for longer periods? The urge to get his fingers on the valves once more was stronger than any fears he may have had. As it transpired, there was no cause for concern, in fact, he found that he had developed a new zest and was blowing better than ever.

The acquisition of the cornet changed Nat's life completely. In those days there was no "idiots lantern" to adorn the corner of most living rooms. On long winter evenings the emphasis was very much on self-entertainment, with friends and relatives dropping in at the weekend for a jolly good sing-song. The front parlour of the Gonella home in George's Road provided the venue for many such get-togethers, with Nat proving to be the star turn with his cornet playing.

It was inevitable that the word would get around about his musical prowess, and he was subsequently invited to join the St. Pancras British Legion Brass Band. The promise of a new uniform once again proved to be irresistible, with Nat duly presenting himself twice weekly for band rehearsals. The band were very popular in north London, and most Sunday mornings they could be heard from the bandstand at the foot of Parliament Hill on Hampstead Heath. At the end of each session the bandsmen would adjourn to the nearest pub to satisfy their thirsts, Nat tagged along with them and on occasion he would find a glass of lemonade thrust into his hands. Needless to say, he was extremely happy playing with the legion band, realizing later that it was a marvellous grounding for any aspiring young musician. It was with this band that he made his professional debut, receiving three shillings and sixpence for playing at a church garden party in Hampstead. By this time his progress was such that he was on the first cornet stand.

The cornet also increased his popularity at work, during slack periods he would entertain the staff. First ensuring, of course, that the boss was out. In a way, this was a little unfair for the kindly boss had acted as guarantor for Nat when he purchased the cornet on terms. On the other hand, what he did not know about, he couldn't worry about.

There happened to be a young girl working at the furriers who had dreams of going into showbusiness, and each week she would buy a copy of *The Stage* and scan it from cover to cover. One day, while she was reading it during a tea-break, an advert on the back page caught her eye, it read: WANTED – YOUNG BOYS AGED 16–18 WHO PLAY BRASS INSTRUMENTS. Anyone who was interested was advised to apply to Mr. Archie Pitt at an address near the Angel, Islington. The girl showed Nat the advert, suggesting that he should try for an audition. Nat shook his head: "No fear, I'm not good enough to play professionally". He cast thoughts of the audition to the back of his mind. But the French couple, who had supported him and given him the encouragement to continue his musical activities, would not let the matter drop, they were convinced that the Cockney lad was worthy of better things.

Anyway, they kept on at him until he eventually succumbed to their persuasion and agreed to attend the audition.

The following Saturday, the stage-struck girl and the French couple made sure that Nat had an errand that would take him in the direction of Islington. After a long trudge he eventually found the address that had been given on the advert, and made himself known to a lady who was representing Mr. Pitt. Somewhere in the background he could hear a band playing but he never saw it. He did not have his cornet with him however the lady solved this by providing a cornet that, presumably, she had borrowed from a member of the unseen band. At her request, Nat played a march, one of his favourite pieces from the legion band that he knew off by heart. His one-woman audience did not show any emotion; whether she was impressed, he could not tell. However, she did invite him to return that afternoon with his own cornet.

It was the Saturday half-day closing at the furriers, but because of the time that he had wasted in trying to find the place, and the time taken by the audition, Nat did not get back until way after 1 o'clock. As he had left at nine and was expected back by ten, the daughter of the boss had waited for him, and promised that he could expect the sack on Monday morning after she had reported the matter to her father. Her words fell on deaf ears, Nat's mind was elsewhere, he was far too excited about his forthcoming interview to worry about losing his job at the furriers.

After dashing home for his cornet, he returned to the audition room where he was introduced to nine other boys, obviously, the band he had heard previously. He was invited to play a march with them, and once again he gave a faultless performance, his experience with the legion band holding him in good stead. This time, the interviewer appeared to be satisfied, and instructed Nat to report to the Alhambra Theatre that evening for yet another interview, this time with Mr. Pitt himself.

Having survived the musical test, Nat realized that everything now depended on his meeting with Archie Pitt, so it was imperative that he should make a good impression. He inspected his one and only suit in the mirror, it had certainly seen better days. Then he had a brainwave, why not wear the trousers of his legion uniform? So, thus attired, he presented himself at the Alhambra in Leicester Square before the great impresario. Archie Pitt was charming, wanting to know about his home, his job, and his musical ambitions. It is also quite likely that he wanted to know why the boy was wearing blue trousers with a gold stripe down the sides, but he refrained from asking. Nat must have provided the right answers for he was immediately invited to join a boys' band that was about to embark on a long tour of the halls. The pay was to be £3 a week – that was big money in 1924. Nat accepted without hesitation, then sped home as fast as his legs would carry him to break the news to mother.

Having secured the job, he did not have to worry about the fate that awaited him at the furriers on Monday morning. As it happened, the boss was very understanding and let him stay for the remainder of the week. This suited Nat as it allowed him to attend evening rehearsals with his new band. Everyone at the furriers was delighted with his good fortune, especially the French people who had been so instrumental in building his confidence for the audition.

The week soon passed, and the moment arrived for him to say farewell to all his friends and colleagues. The furriers shop was now behind him, before him lay many happy years of travelling the world as a professional musician. But on occasion in later years, usually when he was on tour and stuck in a lonely room in a lodging house, his mind would go back to those early days. His French friends, whatever happened to them? And that stage-struck girl, were her dreams of breaking into showbusiness ever fulfilled? These questions remained unanswered.

Nat was certainly not lonely in the immediate years following his debut as a professional, everything was so new and exciting. The troupe went under the banner of Archie Pitt's Busby Boys, and when Nat joined them they were being groomed for a new show that had been written and produced by Mr. Pitt. In order that they should get accustomed to stage routine and the rigours of touring, the boys were taken on a short tour with another Pitt show, *Mr.*

*Tower of London*, but they did not appear in it. This show was a tremendous success, and will be remembered for bringing to prominence the young Gracie Fields who captivated thousands of theatre-goers in the role of Sally Perkins. Gracie had married Archie Pitt in 1923, a union that was later described as a business partnership rather than a marriage.

When *Mr. Tower of London* had completed its triumphant run, the boys went to the Alexandra Palace in Wood Green for a couple of weeks of intensive rehearsal for the new show, which was called *A Week's Pleasure*. Opening night arrived and, much to everyone's relief, the show was well received, the critics hailing it as another hit for Archie Pitt. The Fields family were well represented in the production, Gracie's sister, Betty, played the main role of Myrtle Muggins, and Edith and Tommy Fields added their talents to the cast. Our Gracie did not appear in it but she was responsible for arranging the dance routines and helping the boys with their presentation.

Just prior to the opening of *A Week's Pleasure*, Archie decided that trumpets would create a better impression on stage than cornets, so Nat was presented with his first trumpet – a milestone in his career. The instrumentation of the Busby Boys band comprised drums, one saxophone, two trombones, two tenor horns and five trumpets. Nobody went to sleep when they were on stage. Their repertoire was composed of overtures, and light classical pieces such as "Poet and Peasant" and the "Light Cavalry". To provide some light relief a popular song hit of the day was usually included "Ukulele Lady" and "The Shiek of Araby" being but two examples.

One of the highlights of the show was when the boys performed their guardsmen routine, each of them in a bright red tunic with lashings of gold braid, plus a huge busby strapped to the head. The overall effect was quite splendid, generally producing a great ovation in the finale from the audience. This was something new to Nat, he savoured that applause and, although he was but a mere beginner as far as stage work was concerned, he was eager to breathe in the sweet smell of success that is so essential to anyone in

*The Busby Boys in the "Way Out West" routine. Nat is at the back with trumpet raised. 1927 (Gonella Collection)*

*Archie Pitt's Busby Boys band in Safety First 1927. Nat is centre back row.*
(Gonella Collection)

the entertainment industry. Yes, he was becoming hooked on showbusiness.

*A Week's Pleasure* was booked at most of the leading theatres in the country, always playing to packed houses. They were about six weeks into the tour when the Busby Boys had a change of conductor, the new man being a fine musician named Bert Gutsell. Bert was destined to find fame as the leader of Blackpool's renowned Tower Ballroom Orchestra, but it was not as Bert Gutsell, he changed his name to Bertini. As one may imagine, with a dozen high-spirited young lads to control, poor Bert had his hands full at times. They got up to the usual mischievous pranks and fights that youngsters indulge in, and these minor scrapes generally resulted in Mr. Pitt imposing a fine on the guilty parties. Needless to say, Nat was no angel, he also had his pay docked at frequent intervals.

*Bertini (Bert Gutsell), musical director of the Busby Boys.*　　*Gracie Fields, who was responsible for making Nat aware of jazz.*

A number of the Busby Boys, like those of St. Mary's School, went on to make their name in music. Drummer Max Abrams was a great pal of Nat's and he went on to beat the skins for several top outfits, the list including Carroll Gibbons, Jack Hylton, Sidney Lipton, George Scott-Wood's Six Swingers and Jay Wilbur. Freddy Wood, who was lead trumpeter with the Busby Boys, later joined Bertini when he formed his Blackpool orchestra, and later still became a cornerstone in Big Bill Campbell's Rocky Mountaineers. Big Bill, despite the huge chaps that adorned his legs and the even larger ten-gallon hat that he wore, had horn-rimmed spectacles on his nose that made him look more like a friendly bank manager than a rootin' tootin' cowboy. His main dialogue consisted of "Pass the applejack, Jakey" and "How's about a song from you, Miss Peggy?". Johnny Morrison also played the trumpet in the Busby band, he later became Nat's stage manager when he formed the Georgians, and was responsible for augmenting them in numerous recording sessions.

Apart from her work as a choreographer for the show, Gracie Fields took a great interest in the welfare of the boys, bearing in mind that many of them were away from home for the first time. If she was available when they appeared in a particular town or city, she would arrange outings for them. On more than one occasion hiring bicycles so that they could enjoy a few hours of fresh air in the countryside, away from the stuffy atmosphere of theatres and dingy rehearsal rooms. She also took a special liking to Nat, perhaps detecting that he had a rare talent that should be encouraged. At one time there was even a suggestion that she and Nat should do a duet on stage, the number being "Doo Wacker Doo". Unfortunately, for some reason or another, the item never materialized. However, through one of her typically generous gestures Gracie was to play an important part in making the young trumpet player aware of another field of music, one in which he was to feature prominently in later years – jazz.

This momentous happening took place when Gracie presented Nat with an old Decca wind-up gramophone that she was replacing, and, for good measure, she included half-a-dozen records to go with it. The records featured the Denza Dance Band, an American house band, and a young cornet player named Bix Biederbecke. The beautifully round and mellow tone of Biederbecke's cornet immediately captured Nat's attention, but it was the whole effect that intrigued him chiefly, the melody was being played, but patterns were emerging that went this way and that. He was experiencing the phenomenon we know as jazz for the first time.

From that moment Nat became a record maniac and whenever the show played in a new town he would search out the record shops in order to spend a sizeable chunk of his pocket money on those fascinating black discs. One day when they were appearing in Nottingham, he was standing on the pavement outside a music store when a record on display in the window caught his eye. The label announced "Cushion Foot Stomp", it interested him sufficiently to prompt him to enter the shop and ask to hear it played. This was all part of the thrill of buying a record in the old days, unlike today when most music fans have probably heard the song many times on the radio or television before buying it. The record featured Louis Armstrong on the trumpet, and as soon as it had finished Nat knew that he had to have a copy. The thrill that he had experienced when Gracie Fields had given him those first six records was surpassed by the exciting sound of the Armstrong horn. From then on, Louis was his idol and little could he have possibly imagined on that momentous day in Nottingham that he would actually meet the great trumpeter, or that they would become close friends.

Meanwhile, *A Week's Pleasure* was nearing the end of its two and a half year run. Around this time Nat's newly-acquired passion for jazz was beginning to emerge, subsequently getting him into hot water with Bert. When the Busby Boys reached the part in their programme where they played a popular dance piece, he and Max Abrams could not resist the urge to swing out, their "hot version" of "The Sheik of Araby" producing thunderous looks from conductor Bert, and consequently a severe reprimand after the show.

When the final curtain had fallen on *A Week's Pleasure*, the Busby Boys returned to the Alexandra Palace for four weeks' rehearsal for another new show penned by Archie Pitt, *Safety First*. This show, which subsequently went on the road for eighteen months, allowed the boys more scope. They were called upon to tap-dance and appear in comedy sketches. They also had several changes of costume, dressing as cowboys and indians, soldiers and Canadian Mounted Police with Nat's favourite scene in a western saloon. Their musical combination of drums, piano, trombone and two trumpets being allowed to busk away to their hearts' content without any interference from Bert. They were also trained to move scenery and in one scene that had a nautical flavour the boys had to lay beneath a rowing boat that was placed on rockers, moving it up and down to give the effect that it was bobbing about on the ocean. On occasion the lads would get tired of rocking the boat, their movements getting slower and slower. All of a sudden, they would be prompted into action by urgent calls from the side of the stage, instructing them to put more beef into the rocking.

Life was going well for Nat, he was promoted to the rank of band sergeant, and his pay went up to £3. 10s a week. It is worth mentioning that Archie Pitt made sure that a reasonable portion of his boys' wages was sent home regularly to their parents. Nat's world was complete when his brother, Bruts, joined the Busby Boys straight from school. It did not take Nat long to introduce Bruts to the new love in his life – jazz music. When they were in digs on tour, so that they gave the landlady no cause for complaint, the two brothers played the old wind-up gramophone under the bedsheets, using pins instead of the usual needles to reduce the sound.

The boys' band was a success wherever they played and, when *Safety First* had completed the run, everyone confidently expected that Archie Pitt would present the Busby Boys as an attraction on the variety circuit. However, it was not to be, as they entered the last week, they all received their cards. After four years, the troupe had become a way of life for Nat, it was like being part of a large happy family. What would he do now?

*Young man of music. Nat aged 16.* (Gonella Collection)

# 4

**THE DANCE BAND DAYS.**

*Safety First* played the final week in the Kent resort of Margate, which under normal circumstances was a very pleasant venue for touring shows. But, with the prospect of unemployment looming at the end of the week, the cast of the show, understandably, were down in the dumps.

With three days left to the last performance on Saturday night, Nat sat in the theatre dressing room contemplating his fate. In the previous year or so his musical talents had not escaped interest. He had been approached by several respected dance band leaders with offers to join their outfits but he was unable to make a break because of his contract with Pitt.

Suddenly, there was a knock on the dressing room door. It turned out to be a well-wisher who had heard about Nat's plight, and thought that he might be interested to know that a local band leader was looking for a replacement trumpet player. Nat thanked the chap for the tip and promised to follow it up. He did not hang around, after all, at the end of the week the band leader could make his choice from a whole band.

An audition was arranged almost immediately at the Dreamland Ballroom, this being where the band in question were playing for the season. Nat duly presented himself to the band leader, Bob Dryden, who introduced him to the other members of the outfit. As the fair-haired young man opened his case to produce a rather battered trumpet, all those present at the audition found it difficult to stop themselves from laughing. Quickly realizing that here was an opportunity for a bit of a giggle, Bob Dryden handed Nat a copy of "Swamp Blues", which happened to be one of Louis Armstrong's most difficult pieces. However, they had not reckoned on Nat's musical background; he had been brought up in a stern school and his reading of "dots" was excellent. To their amazement, he rattled through "Swamp Blues" without a hitch, displaying the confidence of Armstrong himself. Bob and the others realized that their first impression of this so-young looking musician had been completely out of order and they were generous enough to admit it. Nat accepted Bob's offer of a job and rejoiced that Dame Fortune had smiled on him yet again.

Working with a dance band was something completely new to Nat, contrasting considerably with his four years with the Busby Boys. He had been accustomed to the paying public remaining fairly motionless in their seats out front and he was now faced with a mass of people gyrating back and forth before him all night. It was disconcerting at first, but he soon got used to it. At that time the country was experiencing what *Popular Music Weekly* magazine described as "dancemania", dance halls were being opened in every town and city, and dance bands were in great demand. Even so, a residency at a venue as prestigious as Margate's Dreamland Ballroom was highly sought after. By joining the Dryden band, Nat had managed to hit the big-time at his first attempt.

The band comprised ten musicians, with Bob Dryden being one of that rare breed of band leader who led from behind a drum-kit. This allowed the front line plenty of scope, which suited Nat nicely. He was able to expand on his leanings towards jazz. Luckily, within the band he found that he had a fellow "hot-music" enthusiast in the form of a trombone player named "Kack" Harris. "Kack" had a fantastic record collection that he jealously guarded, although he did allow Nat to listen to them regularly. Nat spent many thrilling hours listening to Bix Beiderbecke, Red Nicholls, Paul Whiteman and his beloved Louis Armstrong.

Armstrong records were playing an increasingly important influence on Nat's trumpet technique, and he could hardly wait for the next release to reach the record shops. There was one in particular that he would never forget, "Wild Man Blues". He played the record until it was almost worn through to the other side, listening

intently to each note until he felt that he knew it well enough to try
to emulate the sound on his own trumpet. In Nat's own words: "It
nearly drove me round the ruddy bend!" His early attempts failed
miserably, the sound emerging from the bell of his horn bore little
resemblance to that coming from the soundbox of his gramophone.
The Armstrong range was so much higher than his own, and for
some time he had to suffer the humiliation of playing an octave
lower whenever Armstrong's trumpet hit the top register. He even
sent for the sheet music from Darewski's, the music publishers in
New Compton Street which specialized in American jazz. It was not
until the music arrived that Nat realized how much extemporizing
Louis had introduced on to the recording. However, he stuck with
it, and after many agonizing weeks of struggling with his range he
was able to produce a passable imitation of Armstrong's "Wild
Man Blues". In later years he was described as "The British Louis
Armstrong". This never worried Nat, he always maintained that he
was well aware that he was not a musical genius but in his view the
next best thing was to model oneself on the lines of someone who
was.

The summer season at Margate eventually came to a close, but
the Bob Dryden band had acquired a good reputation and they
received an offer to play at the Rivoli Ballroom in Manchester
during the winter months. To add a touch of showbiz razzmatazz
they were billed as "Bob Dryden and his Rivoli Rhythm Boys". The
band went down well with the Manchester crowd, and they managed to do a number of outside gigs in addition to their work at the
Rivoli. By getting out into the local countryside they were able to
experience the hospitality of Lancashire folk, and in all it made for a
very enjoyable six months.

It was during this period that Nat had an introduction to
song-plugging and who better to pass on the wrinkles of this
profitable musical sideline than Leslie Holmes, who later teamed up
with Leslie Sarony to form the "Two Leslies". Holmes was working
at the time for Campbell-Connelly & Co., and he spent many happy
hours singing and playing with the Dryden band. From then on, all
the band indulged in plugging songs for various publishers, selling

copies of the tunes that they played for sixpence a time. Sometimes they sold as many as two hundred copies at one session, the proceeds helping to swell their band fund.

When the six months' contract in Manchester had expired, the management at the Rivoli wanted the band to stay on, however, Bob Dryden kept stalling them, the reason being a more lucrative contract that he was negotiating in the background. The new residency was in Belfast and, although terms had more or less been settled on the telephone, the Irish bookers were insisting on an audition before finalising the contract. This made things difficult; Bob was anxious to keep the matter secret until a definite agreement had been reached.

Bob solved the problem by bribing the caretaker of the Rivoli Ballroom to let him and the boys in the band into the ballroom one Sunday morning at ten o'clock. The band duly arrived for what they thought would be a straightforward audition. However, it turned out to be anything but straightforward. Unfortunately, someone had spilled the beans to the management of the Rivoli. As the band were tuning up, the Belfast booker arrived, closely followed by the ballroom manager. The ensuing dialogue between Bob Dryden and the Irishman on one hand, and the Rivoli chap on the other, was unprintable to say the least. As it was physically impossible for him to throw all of them out of the ballroom, the manager did his best to sabotage the audition by closing the stage curtains and switching off all the lighting circuits in the building. Consequently, Bob and the band played the audition in total darkness. Anyway, they did enough to satisfy the booker, the contract was signed and the ex-Rivoli Rhythm Boys crossed the Irish Sea to play at the Plaza Ballroom in Belfast for the following three months.

Nat enjoyed his sojourn in Northern Ireland for, like the Manchester stint, the band were able to play a number of additional gigs in the area surrounding Belfast. He was gaining in experience all the time, but it was hard work. His musical versatility was useful as, in addition to the trumpet, he played the violin and clarinet. He admitted later that he was a pretty rotten violinist, modestly revealing that he was covered by another chap in the band who could really play well. As the band had to play almost everything from a waltz to a tango, through playing three instruments, it meant that Nat was in every section of the band. He got very disgruntled with this situation because he hardly ever got a break from the bandstand. Matters came to a head one night at the Plaza in a row with Bob Dryden that culminated in Nat raising his violin above his head then smashing it to pieces on a nearby table. As the astonished musicians surveyed the wreckage, Nat calmly said: "Well, that finishes me in the tango section". This was quite a drastic step for him to take, after all, that violin had cost him all of 39s. 6d.

With the summer season approaching rapidly, the band completed their Belfast contract and returned to Margate to play at the Casino Ballroom. For this engagement they had to drop to a smaller band, consisting of drums and piano, two saxophones and two trumpets. They had to work hard for their money, playing three times daily for tea, lunch and evening sessions. For this stint each member of the band received £7 a week, which was good money for 1929, and certainly far in excess of what Nat would have been earning if he had remained at the furriers shop.

Not got to know the personnel of the band playing at nearby Dreamland very well, as they were not involved in lunchtime sessions and they were happy to spend their off-duty time at the Casino listening to the Dryden band. It seemed that their main objective was to hear Nat playing "hot" numbers, and, in turn, he was only too willing to comply with their requests. Several members of that particular Dreamland band were destined to hit the big-time in later years, notably Nat Temple, Maurice Burman, and Sam Costa. In his Margate days, Sam was better known as a pianist, this being before he branched out as a singer, and later still as a radio presenter.

Nat was also dabbling with vocals at this time, naturally basing his style on that of Armstrong. To his personal satisfaction, his efforts were well received by the patrons at the Casino Ballroom, who were convinced that they were experiencing the very best in "hot jaz".

Although life seemed to be swinging along merrily enough, Nat became restless, he was looking for that next rung up the ladder to fame and fortune. He was enjoying a good reputation as a trumpet player and novelty singer and offers from other band leaders came frequently, so he could afford to be selective. After following up an advert in the *Melody Maker*, he eventually decided to join the Archie Alexander Band in Brighton. He said farewell to Bob and the boys with a tinge of sadness, however it was not the end of his association with Bob Dryden.

The Alexander Band had a residency at Brighton's Regent Ballroom, a part-cinema-part-dance hall that was popular with both local folk and holidaymakers alike. When the dance craze was at its peak, the proprietors of the Regent also had the Wimbledon Palais de Danse and the Canadian Palais de Danse, Tottenham in London. Nat brought new life to the band, proving to be quite an attraction. Fortunately, Archie Alexander was a jazz follower and gave his new trumpet star a fairly free hand. Nat set about transcribing arrangements from American jazz records with great gusto, using classics such as Armstrong's "West End Blues" and Eddie Lang's "Freez'n Melt". It was a laborious task, but it paid off for when Archie played the numbers he also had to feature Nat. The band had a talented drummer named Maurice, better known as Mo, who did comedy routines to break up the dance music, and it was not long before he included Nat in his act as a stooge. It was all experience for him but although this new wave of popularity did wonders for Nat's ego, he was still paid only £7 a week.

Nat's brother, Bruts, also made redundant by the break-up of the Busby Boys, eventually joined Nat in Brighton where they shared a room in a boarding house. While Nat was making his name with the Alexander band, Bruts worked as an errand-boy at the Metropole Hotel on Brighton seafront. He managed to get a few evening gigs in order to keep blowing the horn and eventually got himself a permanent spot with the resident band at Sherry's, a fashionable Brighton nightspot.

During his spell in Brighton, Nat had two encounters that were to play an important part in his future, one affecting his private life, the other his work. The first encounter took place towards the end of 1929. In those days it was the done thing for people to visit a coffee stall after a show or night out, especially those folk who were involved in the entertainment world. When his evening stint on the bandstand was over, Nat also enjoyed visiting the nearest coffee stall. One particular night he was standing at the stall sipping his coffee when a pretty young lady caught his eye, they got chatting and it transpired that her name was Betty Godecharle, and she worked as a dance hostess at Sherry's. The meetings became more frequent, romance blossomed and Nat and Betty were married within three months, the ceremony taking place at Wandsworth, London in the spring of 1930.

The other memorable encounter that took place in Brighton was to provide Nat with the break he was looking for, the chance to get into a big-name band. The word was spreading around the music world about a sensational young trumpeter in Brighton who played and sang in the Armstrong style and it was not long before band leader Billy Cotton received the message on the "drums" of Archer Street, the London centre of the musicians' world. Billy was interested enough to take a trip to Brighton, a town he knew well, for in 1924 he had formed one of his first bands, the London Savannah Band, at the Regent Ballroom.

Billy Cotton turned up at the Regent Ballroom during an afternoon dance session, and it did not take long for Archie Alexander to receive the buzz that Billy was in the building. Archie was justifiably proud of his band, so, wishing to present them in the best possible light, he quickly spread the American transcriptions around the music stands. Of course, all the numbers featured Nat. Without realizing it, Archie was supplying exactly what Bill Cotton had come to hear. The following day, Nat got a phone call from Bill in London, resulting in the young trumpeter boarding a train to the capital for an audition. At that time the Cotton band were playing at the Streatham Locarno, so this was where young Nat Gonella showed what he could do. It did not take long and he was offered a place in the band for £8. 10s. a week. Not a fantastic wage but Nat felt that it was a step in the right direction. He accepted.

This move brought Nat back to the city of his birth, something he had in common with Billy Cotton. They both shared that special brand of Cockney humour and, while it lasted, their relationship was extremely happy. Like Archie Alexander before him, Billy also encouraged the young man to continue with his impressions of Armstrong, featuring him in a solo spot in which Nat played "Ain't Misbehavin' ". For this, Nat wore a brown mask over his head with holes cut out at the mouth and eyes, plus a crinkly wig perched on the top of his head. This may sound a trifle crude now, but in those days doing an impression of a negro was quite something, and always went down well with audiences.

There was one particular solo spot in which he was to receive a lesson on the perils of drinking and playing. Waiting in the wings, Nat quickly knocked back a glass of beer before making his entrance. He launched into his version of Armstrong's "Some Of These Days" and all was well until he went to finish on a Top E. He hit the note all right but he could not hold it. After three attempts without success, he slunk off the stage to cry his eyes out.

Playing in that Cotton band of 1930, Nat was certainly in good company, the line-up included Sid Buckman on trumpet, Joe Ferrie on trombone, Sydney Lipton on violin, Mick Burberry on clarinet, Don Whitelaw on drums, and that irrepressible Cotton stalwart, pianist and arranger Clem Barnard.

From the Locarno in Streatham, the Billy Cotton Band moved up-market to the exclusive Ciro's Club in Orange Street. The fact that Cotton got the residency there in the first place astounded most of the musical papers and pundits for it was awfully select and bands were expected to be seen rather than heard. Dining, drinking, and talking posh were the main pursuits of Ciro's, with patrons having their every need attended to by flunkeys dressed in satin knee-breeches and powdered periwigs. It was quite an occasion if any of the club's aristocratic clientele should condescend to step on to the dance floor and trip the light fantastic, an event that usually took place only after they had indulged in enough champagne. In this sedate atmosphere it must have been very difficult for the boisterous Billy Cotton to refrain from shouting "Wakey, Wakey!".

One of the better things to emerge from their residency at Ciro's took place when the British Broadcasting Corporation engaged the Cotton band to broadcast from the club on a weekly basis, thus allowing them to raise the volume and tempo of their music somewhat. The broadcasts also allowed the millions of listeners gathered around their loudspeakers to follow the progress of a young man named Nat Gonella, a name that they would hear many times over the airwaves in the following decade.

Alongside that wireless set, many listeners had that wonderful contraption the wind-up gramophone proudly displayed. This was another medium of entertainment that provided a showcase for Nat's talents, for it was during his Cotton days that he experienced his first recording session. It was to be the first of many. What was the title of the first song to feature the distinctive Gonella vocal tones on record? It is generally accepted that this honour may be accorded to "Bessie Couldn't Help It", recorded in October 1930 but in fact he could be heard as part of a vocal group in "That Rhythm Man", recorded in August of the same year. He also provided a short "scat" solo on the "New Tiger Rag" around that time, the strangulated sound emitted being quite unusual, giving one the notion that Bill Cotton had his hands around Nat's throat, while shaking him in front of the microphone. Nat himself has a different theory about his first vocal record, he feels that he may have made an earlier disc in the form of "Makin' Wicki-Wacki Down In Waikiki", but the passage of time has erased certainty, so we must accept "Bessie Couldn't Help It" as his first recorded solo effort with words rather than "scat". One thing is certain, "Bessie" was a tremendous success for the Cotton band.

Meanwhile, back at Ciro's, the management still insisted that the band should keep a low profile. At times, the music was so subdued one could almost hear the diners eating. When the management asked Bill Cotton if he would be agreeable to swopping places with the band at their Paris club for a few weeks, he readily accepted.

The club in Paris was also named Ciro's but that is where the similarity finished, the atmosphere was much happier and the patrons were decidedly more sociable and far livelier than their

English counterparts. The band were very well received in the French capital, chiefly because they were able to jazz up the music somewhat in the less formal surroundings. Away from the bandstand, Nat and his fellow musicians were also able to sample the delights of the Paris nightlife, or at least what was left of it after they had finished playing for the evening.

Although the Billy Cotton Band enjoyed a good measure of success from the London-Paris exchange, it could be deemed as fairly tame compared with the acclaim given to the Noble Sissle Band who had replaced them at Ciro's London branch. The coloured musicians ignored the management's request to keep the volume low, they went on and did their thing regardless. Amazingly enough, the blaring trumpets and wailing saxophones had an extraordinary effect on the usually staid clientele and many of them discovered what the dance area reserved in front of the bandstand was really for.

It is understandable that when Bill and the boys returned to their residency at the London club, they did not go down well. The patrons of Ciro's, including the Prince of Wales, were now devotees of "hot jazz". After Bill Cotton had appealed to the club management, they did allow him to liven up things. It did not really matter, for the band were not destined to remain much longer at Ciro's. As far as Bill Cotton was concerned, there was one good thing to emerge from the London-Paris band swop, he was able to persuade coloured trombonist Ellis Jackson to join his outfit from the Noble Sissle Band. Jackson remained to become a Cotton regular, and was still playing and dancing when he was in his eighties.

After leaving Ciro's, the Cotton band went on tour for a month, and even played a short residency at Sherry's in Brighton. Although only a year had passed since his Brighton days with the Alexander band, Nat's musical status had grown immensely. In that time he had also become a proud father, Betty having presented him with a bonny daughter, Natalie.

Approaching the summer months of 1931, fate played a hand when Bill Cotton was struck down by rheumatic fever. There were fears that he would not return to the dance band scene but Bill had a tremendous fighting spirit and eventually overcame the illness. That was the good news, the bad being that when he returned to take up the baton again he found that he had lost his renowned brass section – Sid Buckman, Joe Ferrie, and Nat Gonella. Billy Cotton was furious, he never really forgave the trio, putting them in the same class as Army deserters. Nat could not really be certain but he always harboured the notion that the grudge was still there nearly thirty years later when he had prospects of appearing in the Billy Cotton television shows and for some reason or another his guest spot never materialized. On reflection, Nat himself was to concede later that an ambitious young musician is not the most loyal type of person.

From that time Billy Cotton continued a policy of featuring a trumpeter-showman with the band for Nat was followed by such

*Billy Cotton, Nat Gonella's first big-name boss.*

*Roy Fox, whom Nat joined in 1931 at the Monseigneur Restaurant.*

names as Teddy Foster, Jack Doyle and Grisha Farfel. It would seem that Cotton did not carry his grudge to the rest of the Gonella clan for Bruts later joined his front line-up.

On leaving Billy Cotton, Nat, Sid and Joe joined one of the most famous names in British dance band history, Roy Fox. Born in Denver, Colorado, Fox got his first taste of the music world after his family had moved to California when, at the age of three, he sang with the local Salvation Army band. When he was eleven years old, he taught himself to play the cornet and, following a short spell as a bank messenger boy, he opted for a career in music. He progressed to become the Musical Director for Fox (no relation) Film Studios. However, his ambition was to front his own band so when he received an offer to take a band to London for an eight-week engagement at the Cafe de Paris, he was pleased to accept. When this engagement came to an end, he remained in England to hold the position of Musical Director for the Decca record company.

Roy Fox formed a new recording band in the early months of 1931, the personnel of which included pianist Lew Stone, drummer Bill Harty, and singer Al Bowlly among others. Their records were a great commercial success, bringing them to the notice of Jack Upson who, in addition to his interest in the giant Dolcis shoe company, planned to open a new and exclusive nightclub in the heart of London's Piccadilly, its name to be the "Monseigneur Restaurant". Upson wanted Roy Fox to lead a resident band at the club, the financial inducement being such that Roy could hardly refuse.

As the new club was to be something special, a sort of Mecca for the socialite set, Roy thought it desirable to make a few changes of band personnel. This task he entrusted to his drummer, Bill Harty, who was a nephew of Sir Hamilton Harty, the symphony orchestra conductor. He was a very shrewd character, he kept his ear to the ground, and soon became aware of the plight of the Billy Cotton bandsmen when their leader was taken ill. Bill Harty was familiar with the work of Messrs. Gonella, Buckman and Ferrie, not only were they competent musicians, they also combined when called upon to form a pleasant vocal trio. Although they were reluctant to leave Bill Cotton in the lurch, musicians must live, so the three signed en bloc for Roy Fox's new Monseigneur Band. In addition to Harty, Stone and Bowlly, the band comprised Billy and Micky Amstell on alto saxophones, Harry Berly on tenor sax and viola, and Don Stuteley on bass. And of course, not forgetting the musical talent of Roy Fox himself, the "Whispering Cornetist". The Amstell brothers were replaced later in the year by Ernest Ritte and Jim Easton.

The opening of the Monseigneur Restaurant in May 1931 was a splendid affair, it was packed with the cream of society and a number of royal personages graced the occasion with their presence, including the Prince of Wales and the Duke of Kent. The French-style decor of the establishment was truly outstanding with red silk drapes adorning the walls, enhanced by an abundance of gilt. As he surveyed the plush surroundings from his seat on the rostrum and drank in the affluent atmosphere of the place, Nat felt as though he was floating in a dream world, having to pinch himself to prove that it was really happening. His balmy days of youth with the bands of St. Mary's and the British Legion seemed so very far away.

The Prince of Wales, later Edward VIII, was a regular visitor to the Monseigneur and, although he and Nat never actually spoke, they usually acknowledged each other, Nat with a typically British half-bow, the Prince by means of a wink from over the shoulder of his dancing partner. Many patrons were of the opinion that the two men, the musician and the Prince, looked alike and photographs taken of them during that period confirm that there is indeed a facial resemblance. "Georgia On My Mind" was a great favourite with the Prince of Wales, and he would frequently have a card sent to the bandstand via a waiter requesting that it should be played during the course of the evening. One particular night Roy Fox decided to give "Georgia" a rest, so Nat sang and played the "Isle of Capri" for his speciality number. Later that evening he received a card from the Prince stating that the "Isle of Capri" was pleasant enough but he had not enjoyed it as much as "Georgia". The Prince of Wales always appeared to enjoy his evenings at the Monseigneur.

The management of the Monseigneur discouraged fraternization between members of the band and the patrons, any communication between the two bodies usually came in the form of a request card, although it was known for the odd £5 note to pass between dancer and band leader. It was very much a "them" and "us" situation, giving Nat the feeling that he was just another member of the staff, such as a waiter or cook. When they had completed their set and the relief band had taken over for a session, members of the band were swept away out of sight to a remote part of the club until it was time for their next stint. They generally spent these breaks eating, drinking and playing cards.

The typically British stiff upper-lip relationship between dancers and the band must have seemed strange to American band leaders such as Roy Fox, Carroll Gibbons and Bert Ralton, for in the States the atmosphere was far more relaxed and friendly. It is not surprising that one American leader playing on this side of the Atlantic was heard to remark: "Look at them, you wouldn't think that they were here to enjoy themselves!"

During the early 1930s, the wireless was making great strides in the world of entertainment, with dance band broadcasts helping to swell the sale of licences considerably. The Monseigneur Restaurant was rapidly becoming the "in" place so it was inevitable that the B.B.C. should cast its microphones in the direction of the Piccadilly club. In fact, Roy Fox had been in residence only a few months when the management was approached by the Corporation with a view to broadcasting on a regular basis from the Monseigneur. Terms were agreed, resulting in millions of listeners gathering around their sets at 10.30p.m. every Wednesday to hear the plaintive tones of the Fox signature tune, "Whispering", and to hear the man himself announce: "Good evening ladies and gentlemen, this is Roy Fox speaking." Many band leaders had a habit of saying "This is Maurice Winnick speaking", or "This is Henry Hall speaking", as if there was someone going around impersonating them.

In addition to their work at the Monseigneur, the Roy Fox Band also made appearances at the Paramount Cinema in Regent Street, this being in those halcyon days when filmgoers got a first-class stage show with their regular helpings of Garbo, Barrymore, Dietrich and Tracey. Despite their busy schedule in 1931, the band somehow managed to fit in regular sessions at the recording studios. One of the highlights as far as Nat was concerned was "Oh Monah", on which he supplied the vocal accompaniment. It was a catchy number, slightly Country and Western, and it was to hold Nat in good stead some forty-five years later. There are probably still a number of folk around who thought the song related to a girl named Mona but it was a negro spiritual and the title referred to funeral "mourners". On the record, Nat takes the part of the preacher, and the rest of the band are the mourners, the end result being a hand-clapping singalong success for Roy Fox and Decca.

Nat also did a spot of moonlighting on records with various groups in the latter months of 1931, one of the most notable discs being "Swanee" and "I Ain't Got Nobody" with Stanley Black's Modernists, an outfit that included the musical talents of brothers Billy and Micky Amstell and whose pianist and leader, Stanley Black, was only about seventeen at the time.

Through his exposure via club, radio and record work with the Fox band, several band leaders of note considered that Nat Gonella would be a valuable acquisition for their own outfits. The most flattering offer came from Bert Ambrose: he was willing to double the money that Nat was getting from Roy Fox. Who could refuse an offer like that? He had nothing binding with Fox, so Nat signed a contract with the maestro. Ambrose, who at that time was resident at the Mayfair Hotel, was probably Fox's closest rival on the London music scene so it is understandable that Roy was not overjoyed at the prospect of losing his star trumpeter to Ambrose or having to make changes so early in the life of his successful team of musicians. He matched the Ambrose offer. There followed a sort of musical tug-o-war with Nat in the middle but, in the end, he remained with Fox. Nat was to learn later that Roy Fox had paid compensation to Bert Ambrose. This amused Nat, who reckoned that he could rightly claim to be the first musician to have a transfer fee placed on his head.

Things were swinging along nicely for the Fox band, then fate took a hand yet again, when Roy was taken ill with pleurisy in

*Mister nice-guy, Lew Stone, who took over from Roy Fox at the Monseigneur.*

*Ace crooner Al Bowlly, one of Nat's best pals in the Lew Stone Band.*

November 1931. He tried to struggle on but he was forced to take his doctor's advice to go to Switzerland in order to recuperate, living in a small village high in the mountains. With the Billy Cotton affair no doubt still fresh in his mind, Roy was well aware of what could happen when the leader of a band went absent so he kept the band running at the Monseigneur by handing the baton over to Lew Stone as a temporary measure. This was fine with the rest of the band for as well as being a most proficient musician, Lew was a very popular chap on and off the bandstand. Although Roy Fox took all the limelight through fronting the band, it is generally acknowledged that Lew Stone was really the musical brains behind the success of the outfit with his arranging skills.

It would seem that apart from musical prowess, to possess a strong constitution could be a good asset to a dance band musician in the 1930s. Akin to many of his colleagues, when the band at the Monseigneur had played the last waltz, usually around 2a.m., Nat would pop into a late club and sit in on an impromptu jazz session, all for free. The Bag O'Nails Club off Regent Street was one of his favourite haunts and on occasion the sessions could go on until five in the morning. When he had blown all the jazz out of his system, Nat would stagger bleary-eyed out of the club, just in time to see another day dawning. He would then nip into one of Joe Lyons' establishments for a breakfast of bacon, eggs and a cup of tea.

Rather similar to the coffee stall in Brighton, Lyons also served as a meeting place for the "night people", that is folk such as nightclub staff and entertainers, musicians, and ladies of doubtful virtue. It was during one of his early morning breakfasts that Nat dropped his knife and fork for a few moments to take on the role of Cupid. Unfortunately, the arrow in this particular case went way off target. It happened when one of Nat's great pals in the band, Al Bowlly, joined him for a cup of coffee. As they were sipping and chatting, a good looking girl in the shape of Freda Roberts came into the restaurant, and just one look at her immediately bowled Al over, he could not take his eyes off of her.

As it happened, Nat knew Freda from the Bag O'Nails where she worked as a hostess. After prompting from Al, he introduced him to Freda, whereupon the sexual chemistry began flowing like water from a tap. At that time, Al Bowlly had the world at his feet and could have had his pick from any member of the opposite sex that he so desired. Knowing Al's reputation with the ladies, Nat put it down as just another of the handsome singer's casual affairs. To his amazement, and horror, the couple were married within a week. "Oh my gawd!" thought Nat. "What have I done?" His worst fears were realized, the marriage lasted only a few weeks. It appeared that as far as Freda was concerned, old habits were hard to break, and when she said that she would like to keep her friends after she was married, she meant men friends.

With Lew Stone as caretaker-leader, the Fox band went from strength to strength in the early months of 1932, their popularity increasing with every radio broadcast and each new record release.

Records featuring Nat on vocals and trumpet included "Corrine Corrina", "Kickin' The Gong Around", and the evergreen "Georgia On My Mind". Written by Hoagy Carmichael in 1930, "Georgia" was recorded by Louis Armstrong in 1931, and Fats Waller was responsible for a very successful version in 1941, but for British music fans there is really only one name that they associate with this song, Nat Gonella. Nat did rather well with other Carmichael songs, "Stardust" and "Rockin' Chair" being two examples. Hoagy is reputed to have got his inspiration for "Stardust" when strolling across the campus of Indianapolis University one starlit night, while "Rockin' Chair" came out of sing-songs with some of the boys from Paul Whiteman's orchestra on the front porch of Mildred Bailey's house, the rocking chair in question being sat in by the great blues singer herself. As for "Georgia", it is not about the American State as some might think, it concerns a young lady.

There is an amusing story connected with Nat's first recording of "Georgia On My Mind". Evidently, after hearing his gravel tones on the record for the first time, the boss of Decca wrote to Lew Stone: "I think you have spoilt an excellent record by the appalling vocal refrain, if you put out any more records like this the public will soon switch their interests elsewhere." The rest is musical history, not only was the record a tremendous hit with the buying public, it also helped to revive the flagging fortunes of the Decca company. The song will remain with Nat for the rest of his life, even today audiences will not let him get off the stage until he has sung it. So, how many times has he sung it? It is impossible to say, although Nat himself stopped counting in 1938, the tally at that time standing at 5,000. A lot of "Georgias" have passed before the microphone since then.

Despite Roy Fox's fears that his band might be broken up, the line up remained fairly static while he was away in Switzerland. One of the most notable changes took place when Don Stuteley on bass was replaced by Tiny Winters. In the years since, Nat and Tiny have remained firm friends, contact has been maintained and they still manage to meet occasionally for a chat about the old days when they played with Roy Fox and Lew Stone. They certainly had plenty of laughs, especially during their off-bandstand moments on the golf course. To this day Tiny still maintains that Nat was always spiking his ball when he wasn't looking. A great deal of kidding went on among the members of the band, and each was allotted a nickname based on the name of Joe. For example, Nat was known as Joe Soccer because of his interest in football, Tiny was Joe Golf through his passion for that game, Al Bowlly was known as Joe Sex, for obvious reasons, and poor Lew Stone had the title of Joe Clumsy. Lew had a habit of banging into things or tripping up, and most nights the boys in the band half-expected him to step back while conducting and disappear over the edge of the stage. This was rather surprising for Lew began his career in showbusiness as a member of a team of acrobats who were billed as the Australian Sea Scouts.

The radio broadcasts continued from the Monseigneur, allowing Roy Fox to keep up with the band's progress from his mountain chalet as well as speaking to Lew regularly on the telephone. After he had completed five months of his fresh-air treatment in Switzerland, his doctor considered that he was fit enough to return to London. When Roy resumed his position on the Monseigneur bandstand, he could hardly fail to notice that the band had changed tremendously, mostly for the better, Lew had done a marvellous job during his absence.

Just prior to his Swiss sojourn, the band had appeared on the stage of the Carlton Theatre in the Haymarket for a week in conjunction with a film show. They had gone down very well with audiences there and this gave Roy Fox the notion that they should do more stage work. So, when an offer came to play at the London Palladium, he eagerly accepted. Fortunately, the management at the Monseigneur was quite agreeable to the band doing other stage work, as long as it did not interfere with their nightly appearances at the club. However, things did not run too smoothly, the band were due back at the Monseigneur at 9.30 p.m., but very often they did not turn up until well after ten o'clock. This put an extra burden on the shoulders of the restaurant's supporting band, which happened to be Mantovani and his group. Poor old Monty and his boys had to scratch away on their fiddles for some quite long sets in order to fill the gaps. Besides which, the Monseigneur patrons were getting mighty fed up with tangos.

It became obvious that this state of affairs could not continue; the management tried reasoning with him but Roy refused to alter his Palladium time-schedule, he had ambitions to emulate the success of Jack Hylton and favoured stage rather than restaurant work. The management at the Monseigneur had not forgotten the successful and harmonious relationship that it had enjoyed with Lew Stone when he had filled the breach for Fox so they approached Lew with a view to him taking over permanently. Lew was not the type to push himself, initially showing some reluctance but eventually he accepted after pressure from the other band members. They were all given the opportunity to stay at the Monseigneur, Sid Buckman was the only player not to accept the offer, opting to go with Roy Fox when he moved on to new pastures.

Having enjoyed such a successful partnership with Sid Buckman in the brass sections of the Cotton and Fox outfits, Nat was sorry to see him go but Lew Stone provided a more than adequate replacement in the shape of Alfie Noakes, who joined the Stone band from Sidney Kyte. Nat and Alfie made a formidable trumpeting duo, and soon became great friends. Lew also brought in Lew Davis on trombone and Joe Crossman on saxophone, and his own seat at the piano was filled by Eddie Carroll. The full Stone line-up comprised Nat Gonella, Alfie Noakes, Joe Ferrie, Lew Davis, Harold Berly, Joe Crossman, Ernest Ritte, Jim Easton, Eddie Carroll, Tiny Winters, Bill Harty, and Al Bowlly on guitar and vocals. What a line-up, and what a fantastic parade of talent.

Nat continued to make regular visits to the recording studios, playing with bands led by Ray Noble, Edgar Jackson and Ray Starita. In September 1932 he made his first record with his name on the label, "Nat Gonella and his Trumpet", the numbers being "I Can't Believe That You're In Love With Me" and "I Heard". He also recorded with Sam Browne and the Blue Mountaineers, playing and warbling "Sweet Sixteen And Never Been Kissed" and "Fit As A Fiddle" among others. Decca released a record around that period featuring "Eddie Hines and his Trumpet". Who was Eddie Hines? Why, Nat Gonella of course. In those days it was quite common for recording artistes to perform under more than one name. However, it was not Nat's idea to use a *nom de plume*, for some unaccountable reason, Decca decided that Eddie Hines looked better on the label. Anyway, as Eddie Hines Nat recorded "Rockin' Chair", "When You're Smiling", "Sing, It's Good For You", and "That's My Home". On these records as Nat Gonella and as Eddie Hines, his accompaniment was recruited chiefly from the ranks of the Stone band.

The first few years of the 1930s were both busy and exciting for the young Cockney trumpet player, he had achieved so much in a relatively short space of time but there were even busier and more exciting times ahead for him.

*The Lew Stone Band in 1934. This rare photograph shows Bruts Gonella, third from right, filling in for his brother Nat in the trumpet section.* (Gonella Collection)

# 5

BLOW, BROTHER, BLOW.

1932 cannot pass without mentioning an encounter that would remain embedded in Nat's memory for years to follow, in fact, for the rest of his life. It was the moment he first came face to face with his great idol, Louis Armstrong.

Louis arrived in Britain in July 1932 for a two-week engagement at the London Palladium. Fortunately, band work allowed Nat and Bruts to attend all the Armstrong shows at the Palladium for the entire fortnight. Nat recalled how they sat mesmerized at each performance, hanging on to every note that the coloured trumpeter played. Louis was really preaching to the converted, for most of the seats for the first shows of the run were filled by British musicians. However, their enthusiasm was not shared by everyone and although the theatre was packed at the start of each ensuing show, it would gradually empty as Armstrong's act progressed. Apparently, they did not know what jazz was all about. Nat admitted later that he and Bruts took delight in tripping up members of the deserting audience as they tried to creep out up the aisle under the cover of darkness.

As he sat at the Palladium, Nat could hardly have known that one day he would be up on that stage, with Louis watching him from a seat in the stalls. This came about when the Lew Stone band played the Palladium, Louis sat in the front row while Nat sang and played "Georgia On My Mind". After the show, Satchmo went backstage to see him. Imagine the British trumpeter's feelings when his idol came over and said, with that wonderful toothy grin: "Nat, you're my boy!"

It was pure chance how the two musicians first met. Nat hap-

*Louis looking-over "Little Satch".*
(Gonella Collection)

*An historic recording session. Nat with American pianist Garland Wilson in 1933.* (Gonella Collection)

pened to be hanging around Archer Street one day, chatting to some of his pals, when the news came through the grapevine that Louis Armstrong's trumpet was being cleaned nearby in Boosey & Hawkes musical emporium. As he knew the manager there, Nat popped into the showroom to ask if he could have the privilege of delivering the trumpet back to Armstrong when its overhaul was completed. The friendly manager agreed, Nat duly collected the instrument, and set off in the direction of a hotel off the Strand.

In the lobby of the hotel, both the commissionaire and the hotel manager attempted to relieve him of his precious parcel but Nat was having none of it, he insisted that it had to be delivered personally. His perseverance won the day, and he soon found himself outside the door of the great man's room.

He knocked, and after a few moments that seemed like hours to Nat, the door opened to reveal Louis himself. Although it was afternoon, he had only just got up. Despite this, he was most friendly, in fact, he took an immediate liking to this brash young Cockney. For his part, Nat could not believe that it was really happening, here he was actually chatting to his idol. During the course of their conversation, he even summoned the nerve to point out to Louis that if it were not for chaps such as himself doing Armstrong impersonations, he would not have been so well known in Britain. This made the coloured man chuckle but there was a strong element of truth in what Nat had said.

Apart from their love of blowing the horn and jazz in particular, the two men found that they had a lot in common and their lives ran on similar lines. Nat was born in Battle Bridge, a tough district of north London, Louis was born in Battle Field, a tough district of New Orleans. Nat was brought up in a Guardians Institution, where he was introduced to music by William Clarke, Louis was brought up in a Waifs Home, where he was introduced to music by Joseph Jones. They were both influenced strongly through their idolatry for other musicians, in the case of Louis it was his admiration for Joe "King" Oliver, while Nat's enthusiasm stemmed from Louis himself.

The resemblance between the two jazzmen was brought home vividly to British trumpet star Digby Fairweather when he paid Nat a visit early in 1984, it is best described in his own words:

"As we sat in his neat Gosport sitting room, surrounded by reminders of days now long gone, my eyes were attracted to one particular photograph, a dark rotogravure of a young Louis Armstrong, wing collared, with handsome face turned halfway to the camera, trumpet held proudly. 'What a wonderful picture of Louis,' I said. Nat said: 'Look again, it's me.' I looked again, and thought about the profound coincidence of two men born before the advent of radio or television, a thousand miles apart. The shared youth, in a low part of town, in poverty, in a Board school. The mutual urge to play the trumpet, the shared and strangely complementary careers, records played by chance in a shop, and perhaps the most amazing quirk of fate, a trumpet left in a London music store for repair. I looked once more at the stocky man before me, with his cheery face, cratered lips and pert quick sparrow movements. I had to ask: 'Did you ever think that there might be something a bit more than just coincidence about it all?' The old wise face thought for a second, then smiled across. 'Yes, I did,' he said, quickly and finally."

When Nat first met Louis on that memorable day in 1932, delivering that trumpet was not the only service that he provided for his idol. Louis was in a predicament through his cases being mislaid in transit, and at that time he had the one suit only with him in the hotel. Nat solved the problem by pressing Louis's suit for him, so allowing him to attend a reception that had been arranged for him. Louis never forgot the suit-pressing episode, and generally repeated the story to reporters whenever he visited Britain. On subsequent tours, as soon as he placed his feet on British soil, it was fairly certain that his first words would be: "Where's my boy Nat?"

How Louis Armstrong gained his nickname of "Satchmo" has always been a matter for conjecture. Louis himself had no doubts about its origination, in a *Daily Mail* interview during one of his visits to Europe in 1956, he revealed that the name came about through his friendship with Nat Gonella. Evidently, at one of his meetings with Nat during a London trip, he was introduced to journalist Percy Brooks. Nat said: "Mr. Brooks, meet Louis 'Satchelmouth' Armstrong." According to Louis, Brooks, who was the editor of the *Melody Maker* at the time, did not quite catch the full name and said in his very English accent: "Why-er- hello Satchmo." This tickled Louis, and needless to say the name stayed with him for the rest of his life. Well, that is Louis's version of how the nickname originated.

One thing that is certain is that whenever Louis was appearing in this country, he and Nat got together as often as possible, usually finishing what was left of the night, after they had made their public performances, in late clubs such as The Nest, The 43, and the Bag O'Nails. There was also the Jig Club, which was frequented chiefly by coloured folk. Naturally, it was popular with Louis, and he and Nat had some wonderful early morning sessions there, eating red beans and rice with pork chops at two o'clock in the morning. On one occasion when they were there, a whole troupe of coloured dancing girls who were appearing at the Coliseum came to the club. The girls taught them the "Shim Sham Shimmy", and Nat and Louis had a great time dancing around the tables.

Very often the two men would meet at Nat's flat in Shaftesbury Avenue, just a stone's throw from Piccadilly Circus, and spend many happy hours talking and playing jazz. On one such occasion in the flat, they were sipping lager and listening to the radio when suddenly the programme switched to a church service. This did not deter Louis, he proceeded to sing scat all through the hymns. This fascinated Nat, and he would ask "How do you do this bit?" or "How did you do that?", then Louis would show him. Nat learned a lot from these sessions, listening to Louis Armstrong on a record was one thing, but actually being able to converse with the man was something else.

Through their friendship, Louis made Nat a kind of unofficial ambassador to visiting American entertainers by passing on his address so that they could look him up when they arrived in Britain. Nat enjoyed showing the sights of London to such people as Cab Calloway and the Mills Brothers. This was when the latter really were four brothers, John, Donald, Harry and Herbert. John died later and his place was taken by his father, also named John. Those were marvellous days for Nat, he was doing the things he wanted to, and meeting the people he wanted to.

Back in 1933, Nat, and indeed all the other members of the band, had a great respect for Lew Stone for, as well as being a gifted musician, he was also a most amiable and easygoing boss. He was never afraid to experiment with vocalists within the band, and almost anyone could be called on to do a spot of warbling. Al Bowlly, Joe Crossman, Tiny Winters and Nat became universally known as the "Lew Groaners". Lew was always on the lookout for new ideas, ever striving to provide a varied programme of entertainment, thus retaining the interest of the band as well as their rapidly-increasing army of fans.

Comedy routines and numbers were always well received, especially when they were on a variety tour. The saga of "Little Nell" was a great favourite with everyone, and who could forget those classic opening lines: "It was a dark and stormy night when my Nellie went away, the rooster's died and the hens won't lay!" With his high voice, Tiny Winters was a natural for the role of Little Nell, Jim Easton played the poor old father, Al Bowlly was the villain (hiss, hiss, boo), and Nat was the Constable, or "Constabule" as it was pronounced. It was quite a skylark and, although they must have performed the sketch hundreds of times, the players still had difficulty in keeping straight faces. Fifty years on, Nat and Tiny did the "Little Nell" routine at the Gosport Jazz Club and, needless to say, it was still very funny and had the audience in hysterics.

Tuesday nights saw hordes of Stone fans gathered around their wireless sets, or perhaps rolling up their living room carpets in order to dance to the sound of the band broadcasting from the Monseigneur Restaurant in London. Dance band music had played an important role in the rise of the B.B.C., but in the early months of 1933 competition entered the field in the form of commercial radio. The Palmolive Soap Company, which had been prominent as a sponsor on the American commercial radio networks, took the first long-term contract to sponsor broadcasts from the Continent. However, it was the Bush Radio Company which sponsored the first programme to feature complete shows with real performers rather than just gramophone records. Most of the top bands in Britain could be heard on the airwaves via Luxemburg, Normandy and Lyons. Of course, the bands did not necessarily have to travel abroad, the programmes were usually recorded in a London studio. They did not have tape in those early days, the shows were put on to fragile discs, thus making the transporting of them something of a hazard, especially serial programmes.

In May 1933, Nat Gonella went into a studio to record a disc with the renowned coloured pianist Garland Wilson. Originally from Virginia, Wilson went on to New York to make his name on the club and vaudeville circuits. He first came to London in 1932 after appearing in a show in Paris, and while in Britain, he appeared in revue and did cabaret work. Nat had good reason to remember his session with Garland Wilson for it turned out to be one of the fastest recordings he ever made. The studio was booked for 9 a.m., but ten o'clock and eleven o'clock passed and still there was no sign of Wilson. As the studio was only available until 1 p.m., a search was put into motion to try to find the pianist. Eventually he was traced to a hotel, where he was found to be fast asleep. After hurridly dressing, Garland was whisked to the studio, arriving at 12.45. Without time for rehearsal, Nat and Garland recorded both sides, "Nobody's Sweetheart" and "Stormy Weather", in fifteen minutes flat. All things considered, the end result was remarkably good and the record is a much sought after collectors' item.

*Arrival at Rotterdam Airport. The Ray Noble Band at the start of their Dutch tour in 1933.* (Gonella Collection)

In the summer of 1933 the Monseigneur closed for six weeks, thus leaving the members of the Lew Stone band to fill the time as best they could. It so happened that several of them, including Nat, had played from time to time for Ray Noble in recording sessions, so when Ray was invited to take a band to Holland for a four-week engagement, the Stone musicians were given the first opportunity to go with him. Although his best friends within the band, Tiny Winters, Al Bowlly and Alfie Noakes had accepted, Nat was not all that keen to go at first but in the end they persuaded him to join them on the trip. And what a trip it turned out to be!

Air travel in 1933 was still in its infancy as far as passenger services were concerned so it was with some trepidation that the Noble party boarded their special charter plane. They all heaved a sigh of relief as the landing wheels of the aircraft touched down at Rotterdam Airport and managed to regain their composure in time to have a publicity photograph taken in front of the aeroplane. That particular picture included the three musketeers, Nat, Tiny and Al, plus Alfie Noakes, Harry Berly, Lew Davis, Bob Wise, Freddy Gardner and his wife, and Ray Noble with his wife. Although the photo showed a reasonably jolly party, it was noticeable that Ray Noble and Freddy Gardner kept the British flag flying by wearing plus-fours, while Harry Berly was prepared for all seasons with a raincoat in one hand and a tennis racket in the other. Although they were not in the airport picture, Bill Harty and Cecil Norman were also in the Noble party that went to Holland.

The band's destination was Schveningen, a popular Dutch seaside resort, at that time comparable to Bournemouth. The Kurhaus, where the Noble outfit were to play their short residency, was a most resplendent building. It had a very large terrace that was put to good use for the afternoon tea-dances, weather permitting. Fortunately, the sun shone brilliantly for the whole of the four weeks, allowing the holidaymakers to display their dancing prowess and to get a tan at the same time. In the evenings, the festivities and the band moved indoors to the magnificent ballroom.

For the members of the band who had been drawn from the ranks of the Lew Stone outfit, playing at the Kurhaus was a revelation, the atmosphere being in complete contrast to the Monseigneur, thus allowing them to enjoy themselves as much as the dancers. Naturally, gazing at beautiful girls on the dance floor was a popular pastime for the boys in the band, although this practice was reversed

*"Donkey Serenade". The Ray Noble Band in Holland in 1933. Al Bowlly supports Harry Berly's hat between the moke's ears.* (Gonella Collection)

*A jolly beach party at Schveningen. Nat is standing over (left to right) Bill Harty and wife, Al Bowlly, Lew Davis and wife, Freddie Gardner and wife, and Marjie, Al Bowlly's second wife.* (Gonella Collection)

*Gone Fishing! Al Bowlly, Tiny Winters*     *Tiny and Nat, "The Dynamic Duo".*
*and Nat play the waiting game, 1933.*        (Gonella Collection)
(Gonella Collection)

whenever heart-throb Al Bowlly took the microphone for a solo vocal, it was then the ladies turn to ogle. Despite this informality, most of the Dutch Press referred to Al as Albert A. Bowlly.

Taking advantage of the glorious weather, the band headed for the beach in their off-duty hours, sporting a nice line in swimwear that included a vest to cover the top-half, as per 1930s men's style. In addition to this, Nat wore a black rubber skull-cap much of the time, giving him the appearance of Emperor Ming from "The Adventures of Flash Gordon". Prompted by the others, Nat, Al and Tiny provided an impromptu cabaret on the sandy beach, delighting the party with a display of comedy gymnastics.

Through records and radio broadcasts most of the British musicians on the trip were well-known in Holland, and the Dutch people extended a warm welcome to them, both on and off of the stage. However, on one occasion an offer of hospitality was slightly exaggerated, probably due to an excess of alcohol on the part of the host. Freddy Gardner and his wife, Tiny Winters and Nat were invited to spend a night on a houseboat that was moored at a beautiful lake. They accepted and duly took a taxi to the lakeside where they had to hire a boatman to row them out to the houseboat. On reaching the boat, to their horror they discovered that it was more like a boathouse than a houseboat. It was a wreck. However, they managed to get through the night, returning to Schveningen the following morning greatly disillusioned. They were also considerably poorer because of the money that they had to fork out for hiring the taxi and the boat.

Meanwhile, back at the Kurhaus, the high living continued amid the luxurious surroundings, champagne and strawberries being the order of the day. What an experience it was for anyone, let alone a chap who only ten years prior had just passed through the gates of an orphanage to make his way in the world. It would seem that this taste for high living was too much for Nat; four weeks of jollity with an average of only four hours sleep each night had taken their toll, it was a shattered Nat Gonella who boarded the plane for the journey back to England. Unfortunately, as he was the last passenger to get on there was not a proper aircraft seat left for him, so he had to perch precariously on an ordinary chair all the way back. He was feeling groggy enough, this just about finished him and when they arrived back Nat had to go straight into a nursing home for two weeks in order to recuperate from his Dutch trip.

By the middle of September, Nat had recovered sufficiently to join Lew Stone at the Monseigneur for the new season. It did not take the band long to get back into the old routine, and memories of their summer sojourn at the Dutch seaside soon faded. But not for Nat. That excursion to Holland in 1933 proved to be the first of many in the following thirty-five years. In fact, he came to regard the country as his second home.

The latter part of 1933 and the early months of 1934 saw the Stone band adding to their already considerable army of fans via radio and records. Hardly a week passed without one of their records being released to the shops, and what wonderful records they were. Lew Stone's skill as an arranger was well in evidence in numbers such as "Blue Jazz", "White Jazz", "Blue Prelude", "Tiger Rag", "Goodbye Blues", "I Got Rhythm", and the band's signature tune, "Oh Susannah". Records featuring Nat singing with the band included "The Isle of Capri", "Nagasaki", "Emaline", "Judy", "Miss Otis Regrets", "Rolling in the Hay", "So Shy", and the comedy numbers such as "Little Nell", and "Who's Afraid of the Big Bad Wolf?"

Although the volume of fan mail they received from the radio broadcasts and through record sales was flattering, the band did not fully appreciate the measure of their popularity until Lew took them on a variety tour during a break from the Monseigneur. They played in several major cities around the country, the fans turned up in their thousands everywhere that they appeared, and at times the crowd scenes outside the theatres and halls were quite frightening. Of course, many of the fans were women who had come to see Al Bowlly.

The tour proved to be a useful experience for Nat, although he did not know it then. The time was not very far off when he would draw crowds on his own account. In the summer of 1934 he had the pleasure of seeing his name in large letters on the fascia of a top London variety theatre, when he topped the bill with Brian Lawrance and the Quaglino Quartette at the old Holborn Empire. The show was proclaimed on the posters as "England's Reply To America's Hottest", an unusual claim when one considers that Lawrance was an Australian. Anyway, followers of "hot" music packed the Empire throughout the run of the show, the supporting bill of which included variety stalwarts Gaston Palmer and Dick Henderson. The latter was the father of comedian Dickie Henderson, and anyone who was fortunate to witness those wonderful days of variety will recall that he was a short rotund man who wore a bowler hat. After delivering a nice line in Northern comedy patter, he would finish his act by dancing "Tiptoe Through The Tulips" to the tinkling accompaniment of hundreds of small bells which were in his pockets and strapped to his legs.

In addition to Brian Lawrance's violin and vocal contributions, the Quaglino Quartette comprised Frank Gregori on the accordion,

*Topping the bill at the Old Holborn Empire with Brian Lawrance and the Quaglino Quartette in 1934. (Gonella Collection)*

Mark Sheridan on guitar, and Harry Wilson on bass. For recording purposes they usually brought in Jim Easton on sax and Harold Hood on piano. In July 1934, the combination of Lawrance, Gregori, Sheridan, Wilson and Hood, plus the tenor sax of Don Barrigo and Bob Dryden on drums, joined Nat in the recording studio for "Moon Country" and "Troublesome Trumpet". The latter number, which became a regular item in his act, was composed by Nat and a song-plugger named O'Conner in the car when they were driving to Blackpool.

As the summer came to an end, a new season began at the Monseigneur. There were two notable absentees on the bandstand as the members of the Lew Stone Band resumed their places, Al Bowlly and Bill Harty. Through his recording work for H.M.V. with the New Mayfair Orchestra, Ray Noble received an attractive offer to take his musical talents to the United States. He took Bill Harty with him as his business manager, plus Al Bowlly, for the

*Nat Gonella and Brian Lawrance who appeared with the Quaglino Quartette.
These cards were given away with* Radio Review *in 1936.*

Americans had fallen for that special Bowlly vocal magic through
his recording work. Their loss was a severe blow to Lew Stone's
ambitions for his outfit but, being the generous and understanding
man that he was, he wouldn't dream of standing in their way. At the
same time he must have noted the increase in popularity being
enjoyed by his star trumpet player, Nat Gonella, and have won-
dered how long he would remain in the line up of his band.

*Nat in a striking publicity pose. 1934* (Gonella Collection)

# 6

THE GEORGIANS

On Nat's own admission, an ambitious young musician is not the most loyal person to have in a band, and it would be true to say that he had his ups and downs while playing in the Stone band during the latter months of 1934. At one stage he left following a disagreement but returned after a short break.

It was inevitable that he would eventually leave Lew Stone but Lew temporarily delayed Nat's departure by creating a band-within-a-band, thus bringing about the birth of the Georgians. It began when they were on tour playing at the Leeds Empire; the entire Lew Stone band dominated the second half of the show but the first half was brought to a close by Nat Gonella and his Georgians, a group which featured Nat supported by four members of the Stone band. Naming them the Georgians seemed the most logical thing to do for by this time hardly a radio broadcast or a stage show would pass without someone requesting him to play "Georgia On My Mind".

In November 1934, the first records with "Nat Gonella and his Georgians" on the label were cut for the Parlophone Company, the numbers including "Moon Glow", "Don't Let Your Love Go Wrong", "Troublesome Trumpet", "Dinah", "Let Him Live," "Oh Monah", "Sing, It's Good For You", and "Georgia On My Mind". Nat's band line-up on this momentous occasion comprised Albert Torrance on first alto sax, George Evans on second, Don Barrigo on tenor sax, Harold Hood on piano, Arthur Baker on guitar, Will Hemmings on bass, and Nat's former boss, Bob Dryden, on drums. This same group had made "Carolina" and "I Can't Dance, I've Got Ants In My Pants" in the previous month, but

*Nat Gonella's Georgians, 1935, with Harold Hood, Pat Smuts, Charlie Winter,
Bob Dryden and Jimmy Messini.* (Patrick Griffiths Collection)

*Nat blows a hot "Tiger Rag" on the
stage of the Palladium.* (Gonella
Collection)

the November recording session was the first as the Georgians. In the early months of 1935, the line up of the Georgians was subject to changes of personnel including Tiny Winters on Bass, Bruts Gonella on second trumpet, Johnny Morrison on third trumpet, Monia Liter on piano, and Ernest Ritte on second alto sax and clarinet.

Nat and his Georgians continued playing in the Stone stage shows, still closing the first half. Things ran smoothly for a time but Nat gradually came to the realization that certain musicians were only playing with him because they wanted to get a permanent spot in the Lew Stone band. It was then that he made the decision to leave Lew Stone completely and try his luck under his own name. Lew was understanding as always and Nat's departure was quite amicable. His place in the Stone band was taken by Scottish trumpeter Tommy McQuater. Tommy also inherited Nat's band uniform, resulting in fun and games while they tried to fit him into it at Nat's Shaftesbury Avenue flat. When he left Lew Stone, Nat was earning £45 a week. As television quiz masters would say: "Big Money".

So Nat had taken the plunge, he was now the maestro, and he had the responsibility to go with the position. Had he overestimated his popularity? Were the Georgians destined for success, or doomed to failure? These questions would soon be answered; they embarked on their first variety tour in April 1935, billed as "Nat Gonella And His Georgians – Britain's Hottest Quintette". The show opened at the Newcastle Empire on 1 April, and the fact that it was April Fools Day had some significance for Naughton and Gold of Crazy Gang fame were on the supporting bill.

As Nat sat waiting in his dressing room at the Empire, it is understandable that he was a trifle nervous. He need not have worried, everyone was rooting for him, he was inundated with good luck messages from friends and wellwishers, including a telegram that read: BEST WISHES FOR YOUR NEW SHOW, TINY AND BEBE WINTERS. But the most unusual telegram came from a boxer acquaintance of Nat, it said: I GOT KNOCKED-OUT LAST NIGHT, YOU KNOCK THEM OUT TONIGHT, RED. Well, Nat and the band certainly did knock them out that first night, the theatre was packed and the audience went wild with enthusiasm for this latest band to hit the popular music scene. Artistes were paid by results in those days, and Nat probably summarized it best with: "Yes, everything clicked that night, everybody came and we made a lot of money. I came out of it with about £375 for my whack. That wasn't bad was it?"

They discovered the formula for success from the very beginning, and managed to stick to it until the war interfered five years later. Nat was very fastidious about appearance in the act, and both he and the Georgians were always smartly dressed on stage, striving for the clean-cut college boy image, achieved through wearing striped blazers with white flannel trousers. Their programme of music was planned as meticulously as a plan for battle, endeavouring to provide a varied mix that would please as many paying customers as possible.

Before the stage curtains opened, the audience would first hear the sound of a solitary trumpet playing "Georgia On My Mind", the notes getting higher and higher until the entire gathering had one thing on their minds, "Is he going to make it?" Of course, he always did, hitting that top note as the curtains parted to reveal Nat with the Georgians behind him. Thunderous applause. What showmanship!

As the applause faded the band would launch into a light number, followed by a comedy item, then a jazz piece, and finish on a hand-clapping, foot-tapping, rabble rouser such as "Tiger Rag". This number could sell itself, but to lend a touch of showbiz razzmatazz Nat would produce a number of soft toy tigers that were hidden under the lid of the piano, and throw them out over the footlights to the audience. With a bit of luck, they would throw them back, otherwise it was an expensive gimmick. It was all great fun, with the emphasis being on visual entertainment and good lively music. Describing their presentation then, Nat said: "There was always something moving, we never claimed to be a one hundred per cent jazz act, probably only thirty-five per cent of it was jazz. We were a variety act first and foremost on the stage, and commercial was the name of the game."

*Georgian Pat Smuts, tenor-saxophonist*
(Courtesy of Beryl Bryden)

*Georgian Charlie Winter, bassist.*
(Courtesy of Beryl Bryden)

*Georgian Harold 'Babe' Hood, pianist.*
(Courtesy of Beryl Bryden)

*Georgian Jimmy Messini, guitarist and*
*vocalist.* (Courtesy of Beryl Bryden)

The line up of the Georgians remained fairly constant in the pre-war years, a sure sign that they were a happy band, for not many groups stuck together without a change of personnel for one year, much less four or five. As one of the oldest members of the Georgians, Bob Dryden was a good steady influence, and he and Nat made a fine team. Then there was Harold Hood on piano, known by the band as Babe Hood because of his cherubic features. When Nat first heard him playing, Babe was only sixteen years old but he could certainly tickle the ivories. Nat was so impressed with this young man he promised him that if he ever formed his own band Babe was sure of a place on the piano stool and he was as good as his word. He made a wise choice, when one listens to the pre-war Georgians on record it is easy to understand why Babe Hood was such a valuable asset to the band.

Pat Smuts also played a key role in the success of the Georgians, and was considered by many at that time to be among the top tenor saxophone players in the country. As his name would suggest, Pat was born in South Africa. In 1933, when only in his early twenties, he came to Britain to try his hand on the music scene, and after playing with various small bands he was spotted by Nat as a future Georgian. On guitar and vocals, Nat had a fantastic character named Jimmy Messini. Akin to Al Bowlly, Jimmy was something of a mystery man, described by some sources as the son of a Maltese millionaire, and by others as the son of a wealthy Greek shipping magnate, he was also reputed to have gained a B.Sc. at Taunton University, and to have been fluent in no fewer than seven languages. However, there were times when he could not even speak, or rather sing, English very fluently. Jimmy liked a drink, in fact, he liked several drinks. It was not unknown for him to knock back a whole bottle of whisky before going on to the bandstand. Very often, while in the middle of a solo vocal, he would suddenly break out into a spot of unscheduled "scat" singing, which always went down well with audiences. What they did not know was that Jimmy was so drunk he had forgotten the words.

Bass player Charlie Winter was also a colourful character. Although they both played the bass and had similar surnames,

'*Mister Rhythm Man*'. *Nat in his famous Parlophone Records pose*. (Courtesy of Tony Wing)

Charlie Winter and Tiny Winters were not related. They looked nothing like each other, Tiny being short and dark, Charlie being tall and fairish but there was a certain amount of confusion that plagued Tiny in particular over the years. The problem was that Charlie Winter was very fond of the ladies, and had a habit of leaving behind him a trail of broken hearts wherever the band played. Unfortunately, poor Tiny usually got the blame, and if he had indeed sired all the babies that were attributed to him, he would hardly have had the strength to keep his bass upright.

So, this was the basic Georgians stage line-up: Nat on trumpet and vocals, Jimmy Messini on guitar and vocals, Bob Dryden on drums, Pat Smuts on tenor sax, Harold "Babe" Hood on piano, and Charlie Winter on bass. It was a marvellous combination, and proof that "small can be beautiful", a factor highlighted by the subsequent formation of other small breakaway groups such as Joe Daniels and his Hotshots, and Harry Gold and his Pieces of Eight. Another outfit that gained popularity alongside Nat and the Georgians in the mid-thirties was led by George Scott Wood. His Six Swingers included the talents of Nat's old chums, Freddy Gardner, Lew Davis and Max Abrams.

Following their debut at the Newcastle Empire, Nat and the band proved to be a top attraction, with the theatre bookings flooding in. They were also kept busy in the recording studios, completing approximately two sessions a month. Most band leaders were happy to make records, and it seemed that they were not particularly concerned about royalties, preferring to have cash in hand. Nat had the same attitude, usually collecting £75 a time for a session. With the advantage of hindsight, we may now consider what a bad practice this was for surely many of the old band leaders would have been grateful for royalty payments in the lean years that followed. The volume of records turned out by Nat and his Georgians in 1935 was quite staggering by modern comparisons, producing at least 48 titles for Parlophone. Female vocalist Pat Hyde also joined the band occasionally for recording sessions, she was only about seventeen years old then and was known as "Radio's Schoolgirl Sweetheart". Pat, who did an accordion act with her mother in the early days of

*Nat obliges with a few notes for the proprietor of a large record store in Liverpool, 1935. The shop was opposite the Exchange Station.* (Gonella Collection)

variety, still sings attractively, as anyone who regularly attends the "Memory Lane" party nights will verify.

In 1935, Auntie B.B.C. put on her best starched blouse to impose a ban on "hot" music and scat singing. As he was one of the foremost exponents of the latter in this country, the decision directly affected Nat so he wrote a letter to the B.B.C. asking what had prompted such drastic action. The corporation stalled him for some time but in the end he received a rather vague explanation that more or less indicated the ban had been introduced because of complaints from listeners. When one compares some of the strange sounds that bombard eardrums today, and the cacophony that rock and punk groups purport as music, the B.B.C.'s attitude of fifty years ago may seem really archaic but it was quite staggering then the effect that a letter from a retired colonel in Dorking, or a spinster lady living in Cheltenham Spa, could have. This was not to be the last skirmish that Nat would have with the dear old B.B.C.

Around that time a good deal of publicity was devoted to a special concert held in the United States, it was special in the fact that the orchestra consisted of many top American band leaders. In its July issue *Popular Music* magazine offered what it thought would be the British equivalent. The line up was as follows: Harry Roy on sax, Howard Jacobs on sax, Roy Fox on cornet, Henry Hall on piano, Jack Payne on piano and vocals, Billy Cotton on drums, Ambrose on violin, Sydney Lipton on violin, Lou Preager on accordion, and Jack Jackson and Nat Gonella on trumpets. One may surmise that if they had managed to get all those renowned names together for a session, Jack Hylton could have been added, playing the cash register.

The same magazine informed its readers that horse-riding was rapidly becoming a top pastime for band leaders, and went on to say that Nat Gonella was the latest horseman to join Henry Hall, Jack Payne and Harry Roy in the saddle. Nat certainly put a few shirts on the gee-gees in his time, but to actually put his backside on to one, now that was a twist.

In its news column, *Popular Music* also noted that Nat Gonella made a bright appearance in a new film *Pity The Poor Rich*. This film could not exactly be classed as a masterpiece by the cinematic standards of today but for filmgoers in the mid-Thirties films that talked were still something of a wonder. The film opens outside the entrance of a plush hotel, the Georgians enter from the right pushing a large sports car with Nat sitting inside. They are calling "Heave! Heave!" Boys in the band: "We can't push this any further". Nat: "No", turning to Chauffeur, "Run along to the garage and fetch some petrol". Chauffeur: "Yes, sir". Boys in the band: "Queer name for a hotel!". Nat: "Oh! It's called the 'Hotel Encore' because all the top variety stars stay here". Boys in band: "Well, they will appreciate a bit of good music then". Nat: "Sure, come on boys, we'll rehearse the new number, the classical one." The band eventually end up playing an exceptionally fast "Tiger Rag". In fact, it is so fast that a couple of hotel patrons complain that they cannot dance to it.

"Tiger Rag" was used by Nat on a trumpet tuition record that he

*Nat acting the "Superstar", dark glasses and all!* (Gonella Collection)

*Nat with one of his greatest fans, a teenage Beryl Bryden, destined to become Britain's Queen of the Washboard.* (Gonella Collection)

made for Parlophone. In 1935 he also wrote his book on the same subject, *Modern Style Trumpet Playing*. Regarded by many trumpeters as an invaluable aid, the book was responsible for starting several young aspiring players on the road to stardom, including John Chilton and Humphrey Lyttelton. It is now a collectors' item, and is worth considerably more than the original 8s. 6d.

Nat Gonella was never shy when it came to publicity, believing that if you had something to say, then say it loud. To be sure, when Nat and the Georgians hit town, then everybody knew about it. A large display was generally fixed to the front of the particular theatre where they were appearing, it featured a twelve-foot high picture of Nat in his Parlophone pose, wearing his equally famous striped blazer, and brandishing a trumpet while leaning with one knee forward. He also had a lifesize cardboard cut-out of himself prominently displayed outside the theatre or in the foyer. Local newspaper photographers took great delight in taking pictures of Nat posing with the cut-out.

All kinds of publicity gimmicks were employed in those golden dance band years. Just one such ploy to capture the attention of the public was for a visiting band to arrive in town in a fleet of cars, all the same make, model and colour. Jack Payne's musicians travelled in fifteen identical cars, making an impressive sight as they paraded outside the theatre or hall in which they were to play. Nat also used this method of making an entrance from time to time, the Georgians arriving in a fleet of white limousines. The beauty of this form of publicity was that the car manufacturers kept the vehicles serviced and in top condition, it was a great advert for them as well as the bands.

Nat had a passion for sporty-looking cars, his pride and joy being his 1935 Alvis Speed-Twenty, complete with spare wheel strapped to the running board and the name "Georgia I" emblazoned across the bonnet. In keeping with his star image, Nat wore the obligatory dark glasses when driving. When he drew up outside a theatre, the crowd was sure to gather around the car, and when he returned to it he would have to push his way through, bringing cries of "There

*Nat and the Georgians swing-out in* Pity The Poor Rich, *1935.* (Butcher Films)

*Pat Smuts on tenor sax, Nat on his beloved trumpet, and Bob Dryden on drums in*
Pity The Poor Rich. (Butcher Films)

you are Fred, I told you it was him". It is not really surprising that his Alvis drew attention, for at a showroom price of £598 there were not too many of them about. If anyone thinks that motoring was a lot cheaper then, consider that the road tax alone for this car was £12.15s., a lot of money in 1935. Through driving, Nat's career was almost brought to an abrupt halt, just as he was beginning to enjoy the sweet taste of success. He was driving from Wales to the Midlands with Bob Dryden as a passenger when they smashed head-on into another vehicle at a road junction. Nat's car was a complete wreck but, thankfully, he and Bob escaped relatively unscathed. After the wreckage had been towed away, Nat shrugged his shoulders and said: "Well, I guess that it was just my unlucky day." It certainly was, he had been caught by the police that same morning in Cardiff for speeding.

Before 1935 had given way to 1936, Nat and the Georgians embarked on a short but successful tour of Holland. He had fallen for the charm of this country and the friendliness of its people on the 1933 trip with the Noble outfit so it gave him a great deal of pleasure and personal satisfaction to return in his own right as a star name. Concerts were arranged for the band by a Dutch impresario whom Nat had befriended on the 1933 trip, and there was one in which the Georgians had a memorable session with the Swing College Band.

One of the trappings that go with star status is that everyone wants to know more about you, a factor that is well in evidence in the glossy magazines of today. It was not all that different fifty years ago but the articles were not so frank then.

Nat enjoyed his fair share of coverage from the media, becoming a target for writers and journalists from the moment he formed the Georgians. In the January 1936 issue of the *Rhythm Magazine*, Edgar Jackson wrote a highly complimentary article on Nat Gonella, headed "Tailor's Apprentice To Trumpet Ace". Jackson was much respected in the dance music and jazz world, he led his own group The Gargoyle Five, was a reviewer of swing music for *The Gramophone*, and started *Melody Maker* in 1926. His 1936 article relating to Nat included two photographs of Natalie Gonella, aged

*Film still of Nat in 1935.*

five at the time. One of them had her posing with her famous father, complete with a toy trumpet at her lips.

A few months later *Radio Pictorial* magazine had a more personal feature on Nat called "The Girls Who Want To Marry Me". It seemed that Britain's leading hot trumpeter was receiving fan letters by the sackload, ninety-nine per cent of them from female admirers. Many of the letters were written in what one may describe as an intimate style. Nat used the article to appeal to these young ladies, stating that while he was always pleased to receive letters about his playing, the Georgians, Louis Armstrong, or anything they liked about his records and broadcasts, he was not in a position to handle intimate letters from lovelorn lassies. His busy schedule of stage and radio commitments meant that he was working fourteen hours a day. He also made it clear that he was already happily married to Betty and adored their little daughter Natalie.

How did Betty feel about Nat's passionate post? Evidently, the letters amused her and she replied to several of them on his behalf.

She was also Vice-President of the Nat Gonella Fan Club, which one could join for the sum of one shilling. This allowed members to receive a copy of *The Georgian*, a monthly magazine that included news and views on the man it described as England's Greatest Trumpeter. One of the fan club's most ardent supporters was a teenager who was destined to become a top jazz name herself, Beryl Bryden, Britain's Queen of the Washboard.

Despite Betty's involvement in the fan club, and Nat's public statement that they had a happy marriage, their relationship was under considerable strain. In the circumstances, this is hardly surprising; that fourteen-hour working day and the extensive tours at home and abroad that Nat had undertaken in their six years of marriage had taken their toll. However, a man cannot survive on trumpet-playing alone, within a year a new lady was to enter his life.

The Georgians continued to pack in the audiences, topping almost every theatre in Great Britain, including the Palladium. And still the records flowed from the Parlophone stable, in 1936 Nat and the band recorded at least 57 titles. This number included such gems as "Somebody Stole Gabriel's Horn", "The Music Goes Round And Around", "You Rascal You", "Way Down Yonder In New Orleans", "How'm I Doin?", "Bugle Call Rag", "Bye Bye Blues", and "Confessin' ". Apart from Nat's fine vocal on the latter record, it also featured a superb tenor sax solo from Pat Smuts.

Although earlier in his career Nat had been accused of imitating Louis Armstrong, by the mid-Thirties, he was well established as a musical talent in his own right, and other British trumpeter/ vocalists were accused of trying to copy Nat Gonella. Even Teddy Foster was included in this number by *Rhythm Magazine* in 1936. In a review of one of Foster's records, the critic branded him as yet another imitator of the Gonella style of singing and playing, and summed up by suggesting that although Foster was one of the better mimics, he decidedly lacked the exuberance of Nat Gonella.

Nat used that exuberance to take the Georgians on a variety tour with a show called *South American Joe*, a colourful presentation that allowed the cast to dress in Mexican and cowboy outfits. This brought happy memories of youth for Nat, as ten years earlier he

*Nat in 1935, manfully trying to "Hold That Tiger".*

*Nat's musical brother, Bruts Gonella.* (Courtesy of Beryl Bryden)

had worn similar costumes when touring with the Busby Boys. Providing a good mixture of music and comedy, *South American Joe* was a happy show for the members of the cast and the paying customers alike. It would be difficult to imagine a greater contrast than glamorous songstress Phyllis Robins and heavyweight xylophone player Teddy Brown, but both entertainers lent their talents to the show. The blonde and lovely Phyllis was an asset to any production, having graced such bands as Billy Cotton, Jack Hylton, Ambrose, and Carroll Gibbons. One of her popular numbers was how "she and her dawg got lost in a fawg".

Teddy Brown was something else again. As long as there is anyone left who can remember the good old days of variety, his name will survive. Looking more like a giant version of Al Capone than a musician, this talented xylophonist could manipulate those hammers faster than the eye could see. Weighing well over twenty stone, and measuring some 75-inches in girth, it is understandable that audiences behaved themselves when he was on, but after he had demonstrated his musical skills to his own satisfaction, he would bark across the footlights "Sing!". They sang. Born Abraham Himmebrand in the U.S.A. in 1900, he trained as a classical musician but eventually turned to dance music and formed his own band. He first came to Britain to appear at the Cafe de Paris and the Kit-Kat clubs and stayed to become a music hall favourite. It was a great loss to the entertainment profession when Teddy died in 1946.

Nat has fond memories of *South American Joe*, and of Teddy Brown in particular. Despite his menacing appearance, Teddy had a great sense of humour, and once he began laughing it was difficult for him to stop. In the show he took part in some of the sketches and in one scene he had to dress as a cowboy. The sight of Teddy Brown in a cowboy outfit was a spectacle indeed and Nat recalled that during one performance everyone in the sketch got a touch of the giggles. This started Teddy off, in fact, he laughed so much he fell over backwards and was unable to get up again. Eventually, the front curtains closed to bring the sketch to a premature finish, leaving an hysterical audience with a parting view of Nat and the boys

*Beautiful songstress Phyllis Robins.*     *King of the Xylophone Teddy Brown.*

in the band struggling to get Teddy back into an upright position.

The Georgians began 1937 with a new face in the line-up, and what a face, enter Miss Stella Moya, who was also to be the new lady in Nat's life. Of Malaysian origin, Stella was a stunner, her oriental beauty prompting *Rhythm Magazine* to describe her in a write-up as "a vocalist who would appeal to any red-blooded male in an audience". Before joining Nat, Stella was a film starlet, and had the distinction of a fleeting appearance in a Flanagan and Allen movie.

So, she had the looks, how about the voice? As a singer, Stella Moya was no Vera Lynn or Alice Faye but she was certainly comparable with many of the British female vocalists who faced a stage or recording microphone in the late-Thirties. Originally, Nat featured her in his stage act as a novelty item, displaying yet again his flair for showmanship. The stage would be blacked out, then a solitary spotlight would pick out Stella slowly singing "It's A Sin To Tell A Lie" on the side of the stage. Halfway through the number Nat and Georgians would make their presence known by hotting up the tempo, gradually building to a barn-storming finish. A nice touch and guaranteed to make most audiences burst into rapturous applause. "There Goes My Attraction" was the first number to feature Stella with the Georgians on record, made in January 1937, it was the first of many over the following five years or so.

1937 was another busy year in the recording studios, with Nat and the Georgians surpassing their record output of the previous year, making at least 64 sides. A list of the better known numbers would include "Pennies From Heaven", "The Love Bug Will Bite You If You Don't Watch Out", "Caravan", "I Can't Dance, I've Got Ants In My Pants", "Someday Sweetheart", "Bill Tell (William Tell)", "Spooky Takes A Holiday", and "Exactly Like You". To name but a few. One of the more unusual records that they made in that period was with George Formby, it was called "Doh-de-oh-Doh". George appeared in one of Nat's stage shows and Nat paid George his wages. This is how it was in those days, the top-of-the-bill name often had the responsibility of running the show and if it was not a success, they felt the burden financially. This is vastly

*Stella Moya uses her charm on a furry friend.* (Gonella Collection)

*"Tee-hee, Turned out nice again". George Formby.*

different for most of the stars of today, who command huge sums just to appear, whether the seats are sold or not.

Their prolific record output kept the Georgians in the public ear, their stage work kept them in the public eye, and they even managed to pop up in the occasional film. These were British shorts such as *Sing As You Swing, Swing Tease*, and *The Music Box*. Although life was hectic during this period, Nat always found time to help his fellow musicians. His book *Modern Style Trumpet Playing* brought him a steady flow of mail from aspiring trumpeters who had problems with their playing technique. One such plea for advice came from a blind boy, Jack Turland, who was training at the Birmingham Blind School. Nat was so impressed by the young man's letter he invited him to come along to his dressing room the next time that he was playing in the Birmingham area. The meeting duly took place, the blind boy met his idol who not only passed on several tips on how to improve his trumpet playing but also expressed a desire to be kept informed of Jack's progress. Jack

Turland never forgot that meeting, and twenty-four years later he was able to thank Nat publicly on television when he appeared in *This Is Your Life*.

The touring continued almost non-stop. Nat and the Georgians could be playing in a large theatre one night, or in a small village hall the next. The gigs that stuck in Nat's mind were mostly in the north of the country, where poverty was at its worst in the 1930s. While playing in Northumberland, they began the concert with not too many people in the audience but as the music progressed, people appeared to come into the hall in groups, gradually filling every available seat in the place. When Nat had the opportunity to get a good look at the audience, to his utter amazement he found that they all had one thing in common, black faces. It was quite uncanny for the band, looking out on to a sea of black faces. The answer came later when they found that they were in the middle of a mining community, their gradually increasing audience were miners coming off their various shifts. After the show, Nat had a drink and chat with the organizer who showed him a thick wad of payment cards. It turned out that the miners had been paying threepence a week from their hard-earned wages for months in order to see Nat and the Georgians. This deeply touched Nat and made him feel very humble.

Scottish band dates also provided plenty of interest, especially in the Glasgow area. One night Nat and the boys were due to play at a venue in the Barrowland district of Glasgow, which derived its name through its street market association. It was a rough and tough, rock'em and sock'em neighbourhood. The band generally began their show with the Georgians up on the stage, then a spotlight would pick out Nat at the other end of the hall slowly strolling towards the stage while playing "Georgia". A marvellous effect but as Nat looked around the hall and counted the number of faces adorned with razor scars, he felt decidedly uneasy. The management of the hall reassured him that he had no need to worry, a bodyguard would be provided. As the show began, it produced an amazing scene, there was Nat strolling across the dance floor playing "Georgia", completely surrounded and dwarfed by six

*Georgian Bob Dryden, drummer.*
(Gonella Collection)

*The lovely Stella Moya, vocalist with the Georgians and Nat's second wife.*
(Courtesy of Beryl Bryden)

*The Georgians take to the air during a tour in 1938. l to r: Charlie Winter, Harold Hood, Nat, Stella Moya, Pat Smuts, Jimmy Messini and Bob Dryden. (Courtesy of Beryl Bryden)*

huge ex-heavyweight boxers. My, how pleased he was when they reached the stage. They completed the show with the bruisers standing in front of the stage, facing the audience with arms folded.

While still in Scotland, they played a gig in Stirling. As they were playing at another venue earlier in the evening, it meant that they would not get to the Stirling show until two o'clock in the morning. Bearing in mind this late hour, Nat formed the opinion that they would be lucky if more than half-a-dozen people turned up. To the band's amazement, when they arrived at the hall at 2 a.m. it was jammed full of people, with crowds still outside trying to get in. It was just as well that Nat and the band bothered to get there, otherwise the organizers of the show probably would have been lynched!

In 1938, Nat had a memorable meeting with another of his idols from the jazz world, the legendary Fats Waller. This came about when the Georgians happened to be playing at Sherry's Ballroom at the same time as Fats was appearing at the Brighton Hippodrome. In his free time between shows, the great coloured pianist dropped into Sherry's to catch Nat and the band and over a bottle of gin he was persuaded to sit in on a jam session. What a session that was, they only played "Honeysuckle Rose" but it lasted for nearly an hour.

It would appear that almost everybody in Brighton got to hear about the impromptu jam session, including the management of the Hippodrome. They were not amused, taking a dim view of their star playing somewhere else for free, so they fined Fats £50 for breaking his contract. Fats Waller almost exploded in anger, £50 was a lot of money, and represented a couple of crates of gin at that time. The tour almost ended then and there; if it had not been for his manager's powers of persuasion, Fats would have left for the United States on the next available boat.

Although he was the son of a church minister, Fats Waller chiefly worshipped two things in life, jazz and drink. It was his over-indulgence of the latter that eventually contributed to his premature death in 1943 while still in his thirties. Nat would never forget one particular alcoholic tour that Fats took him on. When the bars had closed for the night, the pianist invited everyone back to his hotel room to continue the session. No doubt still haunted by his Dutch binge of a few years prior, Nat took the first opportunity to slip back to his own hotel room to rest his shattered body and to catch up on some sleep. At three o'clock in the morning he was rudely awakened from his slumbers by the telephone at his bedside. It was Fats. "Man, where have you been? We have been waiting for you."

In the summer months, in addition to their weekly variety stint, Nat and the band played Sunday concerts, usually at seaside resorts. They were generally required to give two shows, an afternoon concert at three o'clock and one in the evening starting at eight. As they provided two completely different programmes, many "hot" music enthusiasts attended both concerts. Each programme comprised about twelve numbers, thus giving Nat the opportunity to ring the changes, and a chance for the rest of the band to show what they could do. Apart from Nat's own trumpet solos, the tenor sax playing of Pat Smuts always gained an ovation from the audience in his big number, "Shine", as did Babe Hood with his inspired piano playing on "Sweet Sue, Just You".

The band ran into trouble over one particular Sunday show that they were booked for at the Odeon Theatre at Hanley, Staffordshire. Entertainment of any sort on the Lord's Day was still frowned on in some quarters, and theatre managers were required to apply for a special licence from their local magistrates. The manager of the Hanley Odeon, a Mr. Harris, had to appear before a magistrate with a copy of the Georgians intended Sunday programme. "I have heard this 'I Yi Yi Yi' song before," said the magistrate, "it is certainly not suitable to play on a Sunday." Mr. Harris produced a pencil and deleted the number from his list. "And what is this item, 'Booglie, Wooglie, Piggy'? Oh dear no!" said the magistrate. Mr. Harris used his pencil yet again. Then the old gent almost fell off the bench, gazing incredulously over the top of his glasses he uttered: " 'A Flat Foot Floogie With A Floy Floy'. Out!" By the time that he had gone through the list, Mr. Harris was looking for a pencil sharpener and about all the band had left on the programme was "God Save The King".

*Nat in drag for the* King Revel *show at Blackpool in 1938.* (Gonella Collection)

*Looking like a refugee from the* Chocolate Soldier, *Nat in a scene from* King Revel. (Gonella Collection)

One of the highlights of 1938 for Nat and his group was when they were invited to do a summer season at the Blackpool Hippodrome. Produced by Jack Taylor, this seaside spectacular was called *King Revel*, the cast list included Sandy Powell, Norman Evans and Duggie Wakefield. The show really was spectacular in the best Busby Berkeley style, and in one scene there was a magnificent glass stairway adorned with lots of beautiful showgirls posing in splendidly colourful costumes. *King Revel* broke the Hippodrome's box-office record the first night, with over 3,000 people in the audience. It was a marvellous experience for every member of the band, Nat appeared in some of the comedy sketches and Stella sang in some of the show's biggest and most lavish scenes. Most of the music in *King Revel* was specially written for it by that prolific songwriter, Horatio Nicholls.

As a permanent reminder of his pleasant sojourn in Blackpool

Nat and the band went into the recording studio to cut "The Blackpool Walk". During the same session in July 1938, they also made a record of the "Lambeth Walk", which was very popular at the time. Written by Noel Gay, the song was used extensively by Lupino Lane, who took exception to it being used in other shows, for it was the highlight of his own show at the Victoria Palace, London, *Me And My Girl*. Lane's solicitors sent out letters of warning to various theatrical producers, stating that action would be taken against them if they used the song. In November 1938, Nat Gonella, who was appearing at the Gaumont in Holloway, London, at the time, received a letter from Lupino Lane assuring him that the ban on the "Lambeth Walk" was not intended for him, and that he was grateful for Nat's help in popularizing the song. Lane concluded by stating that he hoped that Nat would continue to use it whenever he wished. So Nat carried on doing the "Lambeth Walk".

As 1938 was drawing to a close, Nat took time to pause and reflect on what a marvellous year it had been for him and indeed on how successful life had been since he had formed the Georgians. Many of the entertainers to whom he had played host on their visits to Britain from the States had indicated that he would be most welcome if ever he should make the trip across the Atlantic. It was true that for many years Nat had nourished a dream that one day he would be in a position to visit America, the home of jazz.

Theatres were getting ready for the pantomime season, his bank balance looked healthy, so it seemed as opportune a time as any to make his American dream come true.

# 7

THE AMERICAN DREAM.

*Nat in about 1938.*

*Harry James, one of the nicest people that Nat met on his American trip.*

In those balmy days of peace before World War II, the power of radio, records and films had made the names of British band leaders famous all over the world, even in non-English speaking countries. Imagine the surprise of a party of English tourists travelling through Hungary when they stopped at a small village petrol station, they were greeted by shouts of "Harry Roy" from the natives. Evidently, the Hungarians had an unusual interpretation of "English spoken here": their way of saying hello was to pump the visitors' hands vigorously and exclaim loudly "Harry Roy". So, if "Harry Roy" meant hello, what did they say for goodbye? Would you believe "Nat Gonella"? Just imagine the scene as the tourists drove away from the petrol station, with the natives waving their arms like mad and shouting "Nat Gonella" at the tops of their voices.

British musicians and entertainers were also making their mark in America, both Ray Noble and Al Bowlly had tasted the fruits of success over there so Nat Gonella was anxious to discover what the American music scene was all about. Primarily, it was his intention that the trip should be a holiday, however, it turned out to be anything but.

On a grey December day in 1938 the SS *Hamburg* sailed out of Southampton, bound for New York. Nat and Stella had just received a great send-off from the boys in the band, as it was only three days to Christmas, they had presented Nat with a gold ring. Unfortunately, it was not a very happy crossing, most of the other passengers were refugees and the weather was atrocious. This did not worry Nat too much as he proved to be a good sailor.

On the second day out he made the acquaintance of Timme Rosenkrantz, a Danish journalist who wrote for a music magazine in Denmark. Timme had brought some records on the voyage but he did not have anything to play them on so he and Nat searched the German liner high and low for a gramophone. Eventually, their perseverance was rewarded, they found that the only record player on board was kept behind the bar. Every evening from then on, after the refugees had retired to their cabins to dream of the life that lay ahead of them in a new country, the music-loving pair took over the bar for long record sessions way into the night.

The outstanding skyline of New York came into view on 29 December but by the time that the *Hamburg* had docked it was eight o'clock in the evening. Nat and Stella booked in at the Hotel Piccadilly on Forty Fifth Street, just off Broadway. Most travellers would have been content to have an early night in order to be fresh for sightseeing the next day but not Nat, he had waited a long time for this trip and he was determined to make the most of every moment. After donning their glad rags, they went out on the town.

For his first taste of live music in America, they merely took the lift down to the Hotel Piccadilly's fabulous Georgia Room. The resident group there was led by renowned bass saxophonist Adrian Rollini, supported by vibraphone, guitar and bass. They made a great sound, leaving Nat suitably impressed. Rollini was America's first exponent of the bass sax, an instrument not heard all that often in jazz nowadays, apart from Britain's own expert, jazz veteran Harry Gold.

Moving on from the hotel, Nat and Stella popped into the Paramount Cinema to see Glen Gray and the Casaloma Orchestra with the Andrews sisters. Then, from the Paramount they went to the Famous Door Club on Fifty Second Street, a mecca for jazz in New York. John Kirby and his band were playing music for dancing there and the Red Norvo Band with singer Mildred Bailey were also on hand. Surprisingly, Nat was rather disappointed so they left to sample the musical delights of the Savoy Ballroom in Harlem, where multi-instrumentalist Don Redman was playing with his band. The relief band at the Savoy, the Savoy Sultans, were also playing. Nat preferred them to the Redman outfit, their brass section being outstanding in his opinion. Then they returned to the Hotel Piccadilly, eventually climbing into bed at five o'clock in the morning. Not bad for their first night in America.

The next day, or perhaps we should say later that day, Nat's first call was to look up his old pal Tommy Farr, the British heavyweight boxing champion. Tommy will be remembered as one of only three fighters who went the distance with Joe Louis, and although the "Brown Bomber" emerged as the victor on that occasion, many thought that the Welshman had done enough to win this epic contest. Tommy stayed on in the States hoping to get a return fight with Louis but it was not to be; when he eventually returned to Britain, he had lost all of his five bouts in America. Anyway, he was pleased to see Nat, and the two of them went to Madison Square Gardens to watch the fights. Tommy was in training at the time for his forthcoming fight with Red Burman, a protégé of Jack Dempsey, so he was unable to stay out too late. After he had said goodnight to Tommy, Nat went on to the Cotton Club in Harlem to enjoy a feast of good jazz provided by Cab Calloway and his band. Nat was particularly taken with the drummer in Cab's splendid outfit, Cozy Cole, who was later destined to become one of Louis Armstrong's All-Stars. The supporting acts included the Nicholas Brothers and the Berry Brothers, Sister Rosetta Tharpe with her choir of twenty singers, and the great W.C. Handy. Nat recalled that Handy was almost blind and had to be led on to the stage where he played his own composition, "St. Louis Blues", on the trumpet. And so the second night of his American trip over, Nat opted for an early night – 4 a.m.

In the late 1930s, vaudeville was experiencing something of a revival in America, so Nat decided that he would like to see a show so that he could compare it with British variety. As it transpired, he was quite impressed, which is not surprising when one considers that the bill included Fats Waller and Myra Johnson. Nat thought that Fats gave a far better performance he had provided on his British tour a few months earlier.

Following their taste of American vaudeville, Nat and Stella went on to the Waldorf Astoria to see in the New Year. Benny Goodman was playing at the Waldorf and Nat was given the opportunity to meet him as the evening progressed. He also met several of the top-notch musicians who were playing with Benny, including trumpet ace Harry James, pianist Teddy Wilson and vibes player Lionel Hampton. Nat found Harry James to be a rather quiet and reserved sort of chap, and one of the nicest people that he met on the trip. The night did not end at the Waldorf Astoria; Nat returned to Harlem to see the Jimmy Lunceford Band at the Renaissance Ballroom, his main objective being to hear Lunceford's star trumpeter, Cy Oliver, who later in 1939 left to join Tommy Dorsey. Satisfied that he had seen the New Year well and truly in, Nat eventually fell into his bed at 6 a.m.

He awoke in the afternoon, just in time to visit a nearby cinema. The film show included a live stage presentation featuring Abe

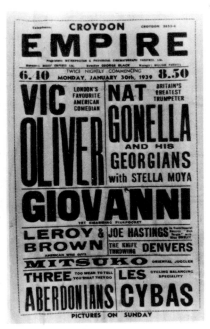

*A snapshot of Nat taken on his American trip.*

Lyman and his renowned band. Returning to the hotel, Nat thought that it would be wise to close his eyes for an hour or so before going out on the town for another evening of jollity and music. It was then that the hectic pace of the previous three days hit him, he did not wake up until two o'clock the following afternoon. What is more, he still had his trousers on!

Of course, Nat could not let his trip to America pass without seeing his old friend Louis Armstrong. He caught up with Satchmo at a combined movie-stage show at the Strand Theatre to promote his latest film, *Goin' Places*. Appearing on stage with the Luis Russell Orchestra and Bill Robinson, Louis was playing as well as ever, although Nat could not help but notice that he had put on a considerable amount of weight since he had last seen him in Britain. Anyhow, Louis was pleased to see Nat again and made him very welcome.

It is not desirable for a trumpeter to be parted from his mouth-piece for too long, so Nat was grateful for any opportunity he had to have a blow. He was able to spend many enjoyable hours playing his horn at Nick's Tavern, in New York's Greenwich Village. For the price of a drink, one could wallow in some of the hottest music in town at Nick's. Bobby Hackett and his orchestra were resident there during Nat's stay and the relief band was Sidney "Pops" Bechet and his Bluebloods. Nat formed the opinion that Hackett's trumpet playing was as near to the sound of Bix Beiderbecke as one was likely to hear, and he was absolutely knocked out by the soprano sax playing of "Pops" Bechet. It is worth mentioning that the legendary "Zutty" Singleton was playing the drums with Bechet at the time. So when Nat was invited to join these bands on the stage, he was in fine company.

On one particular evening at Nick's Tavern, it transpired that Bobby Hackett was plagued by gumboils and was unable to play so Nat filled in for him. While he was playing, trumpeter Wingy Manone dropped by and joined him for a memorable session. Apart from Wingy Manone's one-handed playing technique, Nat was quite astounded by the quantity of drink that he consumed in a relatively short time; it seemed that Wingy's idea of warming-up before a session was to knock back eight scotches in a row. What a session that turned into, with Nat eventually falling into bed at 5 a.m.

Another great night that Nat would savour for years to follow took place at the New Yorker Hotel, this was when Jimmy Dorsey took over the residency from his brother Tommy. The Dorseys were tremendously popular and the ballroom was packed with film-stars and celebrities. Count Basie was another star name that he was eager to see but he had to travel to Philadelphia to fulfil this objective.

Nat was sitting in a club one night when he spotted Fats Waller entering the place. He half-stood to offer his hand but Fats walked straight past, ignoring him completely. However, a couple of hours later Fats came over to his table and greeted Nat like a long-lost brother. "You're a funny bugger," said Nat. "When you first came in you ignored me." Fats merely beamed and said: "Ah yes, but then I was cold sober. I never recognize anyone until I've got a few drinks under my belt."

In another club Nat met Joe Marsala, with whom he hit it off immediately and the result was another great jam session. By this time the word was beginning to get around about the dynamic trumpeter from England who could blow with the best of them so it was inevitable that he should receive plenty of offers of work if he should decide to settle in the States. It was obvious that he could make a lot of money if he did indeed take this important step. It was awfully tempting, it meant that he could play the kind of music that he really wanted to. After giving the matter some thought, Nat made the decision to put the official wheels in motion with a view to becoming an American citizen. Of course, it was not quite so easy as that, there were a great number of forms to complete and interviews to be negotiated but at least he had made a start to the lengthy procedure required by the immigration authorities in the States.

The latter half of his American holiday was as hectic as the first half, in many ways it was even more so for almost every club that he visited expected him to join the band on the rostrum. The musicians who he saw, met, and very often played with reads like a Who's Who of jazz, including Duke Ellington, Artie Shaw, Chick Webb, Noble Sissle, Billie Holliday, Claude Hopkins, Teddy Hill, Roy Eldridge, Joe Venuti, Ben Webster, Dickie Wells, Johnny Mercer, Red McKenzie, Pee-Wee Russell, Glenn Miller, Phil Napoleon, and many more.

Nat would never forget his last full day in New York, it provided a wonderful finale for his holiday. He had a permanent reminder of the trip in the form of an historic recording session with a band of all-stars led by John Kirby. In addition to Nat's vocals and inspired trumpet playing, the group comprised Buster Bailey on clarinet, Benny Carter on alto sax, Billy Kyle on piano, Brick Flegal on guitar, Jack Mussell on drums, and John Kirby on bass. The end product was four excellent sides, "You Must Have Been A Beautiful Baby", "A Kid Named Joe", "Jeepers Creepers", and "I Must See Annie Tonight". The last number is particularly notable in that it highlights the famous Gonella lisp, with "Operator give me a line" emerging as "Oper-waiter give me a line". This was a unique aspect of his singing that was exploited over the years by record producers, "Stardust" being but one example. A sidelight to his American recording was that in order to satisfy the strict rules laid down by the Musician's Union, Nat had to pay an American musician 35 dollars just to sit-in on the session, not to play, but to merely sit there while Nat was blowing.

Nat and Stella spent their last night in New York at the Cotton Club with Tommy Farr, having seen Tommy lose his fight against Burman a week earlier. Tommy also had his bodyguard with him at the club. It may seem strange that a heavyweight boxer should need a bodyguard but that was the state of the fight game in the States, gangsters and gambling well in evidence and a boxer could often earn more money by losing than winning. Sadly, racketeers also had some control on the music scene through their interests in night-clubs.

The Cotton Club was packed with celebrities that night, who were there to say farewell to Abe Lyman who was taking his band to Miami for the season. The distinguished gathering included the Andrews Sisters, (Patty, Maxene and La Verne) who were still basking in the success of their first big hit "Bei Mir Bist Du Schoen". The Mills Brothers were also there, and pleased to see Nat again. In addition to Tommy Farr, there were several other boxers in the audience, including Joe Louis and Max Baer.

The main music of the evening was provided by Cab Calloway and his band but at intervals stars from the audience were invited to the bandstand to do a turn. At one stage Tommy Farr was called out and introduced to the assembly. Tommy promised them that he would not sing but he did add that he would like them to meet a bandleader friend of his from England. The crowd clapped politely as Nat stepped up to the stage. On the other hand, Cab Calloway and his boys were absolutely delighted to see Nat again for they had fond memories of him from their trip to Britain. Before he knew what was happening, someone had thrust a trumpet in his hands. Nat admitted later that he was as nervous at that moment as at any time in his life, and who wouldn't have been before such a gathering of showbiz stars?

The nerves vanished as he placed the horn to his lips and launched into "Ain't Misbehavin' ". When he had finished, the response from the audience was tremendous, but they did not show their appreciation by clapping, they used small hammers provided by the management to tap their tables. The noise was terrific, Nat thought that World War II had begun in earnest. In answer to the cries of "encore", he obliged with "Old Man Mose".

When they finally allowed Nat to return to his table, he hardly had need of the drink that was awaiting him, he was sufficiently intoxicated by the acclaim given to him by the wildly enthusiastic audience. Towards the end of the evening, Tommy Farr's body-guard introduced Nat to the owner of the Cotton Club, who also happened to be the manager of World Champion Joe Louis, and was reputed to have connections in the gangster underworld. Anyway, he was impressed by Nat's performance and made him an offer to appear at the 1939 World's Fair, to be held in New York. The same evening Nat had been approached by Abe Lyman to sign a contract with him. So if his naturalization papers went through all right and the American Musician's Union gave its blessing, he was assured of plenty of work on his return to the States.

The following day, 21 January, Nat and Stella said goodbye to their American friends and sailed for Britain. As the liner steamed out of New York Harbour, he could not help but wonder how long it would be before he returned. However, Nat had not reckoned with the war clouds that were gathering over Europe. His papers for naturalization were never finalized and his American dream faded to become a memory of what might have been.

# 8

# A TRUMPETER AT WAR.

On their return from the United States, Nat and Stella hardly had time to unpack their cases, embarking almost immediately on a Moss Empires variety tour with the Georgians. They shared top billing with comedian Vic Oliver, who was destined to become a household favourite in the popular radio show "Hi Gang" with Bebe Daniels and Ben Lyon.

Despite the hectic tour, Nat still found time to go to the horse races. In March, 1939, the *Daily Sketch* featured Stella Moya wearing the latest fashion for lady racegoers, complete with a

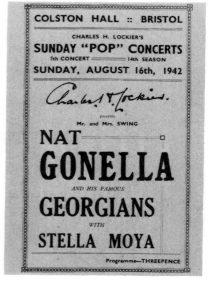

photograph of her wearing a smart kidskin coat with a matching handbag. But it was her net cap with beaver ear muffs that really made the fashion correspondent go into raptures. We cannot be certain if Nat even noticed what Stella was wearing at the races, he was probably too busy studying form. Bookmakers and betting offices were very pleased with Nat's patronage over the years, but although he lost a few shirts in his time, his gambling was never in the same class as Ambrose. The story about how Ambrose lost over £20,000 in one night at the Monte Carlo gaming tables is now legendary.

While the *Daily Sketch* was interested in what Stella was wearing, the *Rhythm Magazine* in 1939 was more intent on divulging Nat Gonella's stage habits. In an article concerning the individual idiosyncrasies of band leaders, it was revealed that Benny Goodman always gave a tweak to each end of his bow-tie before going on stage to perform, Tommy Dorsey always moved his trombone slide up and down as if he was checking that it was well oiled, and Nat Gonella had a habit of looking down at his fingernails. Forty years on, when called upon to provide one of his unique vocals, Nat still looks down at his outstretched fingernails while waiting between choruses.

In June 1939, Nat had an honour bestowed on him by fellow members of his profession when he was selected to act as a judge for the All-Britain Dance Band Championships at the Winter Gardens in Blackpool. With the other members of the judging panel, Geraldo, George Elrick, Art Strauss and Bram Martin, he listened to a total of 38 top bands. Quite a marathon. The bands battled it out for the coveted Jack Hylton Gold Cup, which was won that year by the Billy Lawrence Band from London.

Although their record output was not so high in 1939 as it had been in the previous four years, Nat and the Georgians made several sides that were interesting and typical of the immediate pre-war period. They included "Hold Tight", "Tain't What You Do", "One o'clock Jump", "Boogie Woogie", and the charming "Three Little Fishes" which featured the combined vocal talents of Nat and Stella. The voice of Jimmy Messini also came over well in "South of the Border" and "Deep Purple", a mixture of Monte Rey and Alan Jones.

On 15 August, the band embarked on a tour of Sweden. Taking in Stockholm and other large centres, it was their second visit to this country. On their previous tour they had played mostly in small towns and on one occasion they travelled all night to reach their destination, where they found that their concert hall was a small schoolhouse. Despite this, all the members of the band liked the country and had fond memories of the hospitality given to them by the Swedish people. Stella was particularly excited at the prospect of a return tour for she was the only honorary lady member of the Swedish Musicians Union, an honour bestowed on her during the first trip.

The Swedish tour was very successful and they even managed to get into Holland for a few concerts. In Amsterdam they gave a Royal performance for Prince Bernhardt, a show that Nat would not forget in a hurry. He was anxious that the concert should go well, wishing to make a good impression. The thing that worried him most was Jimmy Messini's drinking so he had a heart-to-heart chat with Jimmy that ended with him promising Nat faithfully that he would lay off the alcohol.

The first half of the show went through without any hitches. At one stage in their programme Nat had the opportunity to whisper to Jimmy: "Everything okay, Jimmy?" Jimmy nodded: "Sure Nat, but I am terribly dry. I could sure use a drink!" Nat relented. "Okay Jimmy, I'll arrange with a waiter to have one ready for you in the wings." He was as good as his word, a glass of schnapps was waiting for Jimmy. Unfortunately, the tumbler was full to the brim with the Dutch gin. This was bad enough but what Nat did not know was that the crafty Jimmy already had knocked back his customary bottle of whisky before the show. He had enough Dutch courage to drive a windmill.

In the second half, Jimmy was due to sing one of his big numbers, "Donkey Serenade". The moment for his vocal solo arrived and Nat announced: "Your Royal Highness, ladies and gentlemen, my vocalist Jimmy Messini will now sing that popular number, 'Donkey

Serenade'." The band struck up, Jimmy got up from his seat, took two steps forward, and fell flat on his face, out to the world. Nat grabbed the microphone: "Your Royal Highness, ladies and gentlemen, I am awfully sorry about this, I am afraid that my singer has been overcome by nerves through having to appear before such a distinguished audience." Cries of sympathy went around the hall and as Jimmy Messini was carried off the stage, they applauded him.

Although their 1939 tour began well enough, it had an ending that none of the Georgians envisaged. Adolf Hitler's evil war machine was getting into first gear, and sea and air connections between Britain and the Continent were suspended, leaving thousands of Britons stranded. Several entertainers were left out on a limb: Will Hay was trying to get out of Norway, Bobby Howes and his family were stuck in France, and Nat and the Georgians were kicking their heels between Sweden and Holland.

One day, Nat and Babe Hood were sitting by a bandstand contemplating their lot when Nat remarked: "Cor! If I only had wings." Babe looked up and said: "That sounds like a great title for a song to me." He promptly sat down at the piano and between them they composed a chirpy little ditty that was indeed called "If I Only Had Wings". They recorded the number in Stockholm with the Thore Ehrling Orchestra on 13 September, on the Odeon label, with "Sunrise Serenade" on the reverse side. Ehrling was also a crack trumpeter and ran the most successful Swedish dance band at that time. The record included three trumpets, Thore, Nat, and Bruts Gonella, who was also on the tour with the Georgians on the trip. The piano playing of Babe Hood also comes through loud and clear on the "If I Only Had Wings" side of the record. Unfortunately, when they did eventually get back to England with the song, there was another already published under the same title. The music publishers bought Nat's version, and promptly put it on the shelf. A great shame, for when one hears the number now it has a catchy quality.

Meanwhile, the Germans were getting into second gear, and surprisingly enough, anti-British propaganda was quite high in

Holland. The band frequently had requests to play German numbers but Nat always refused. With Hitler knocking even harder on the door, the Georgians had to split up and make their way home as best they could. Nat and Stella managed to get out of Holland with only days to spare before the Germans marched in, fleeing to the South of France to join a group of Britons who were also stranded and waiting hopefully for the British Government to send a rescue boat.

The Italians bombed Cannes and the situation was getting desperate. Suddenly, a rescue vessel appeared on the horizon, it would be able to take them to Gibraltar at least. Tired and weary, Nat and Stella got on board the boat, all they had was what they were wearing, plus a dress suit and Nat's trumpet. All their other possessions, including some £600, lay sprinkled through Sweden, Denmark, Holland and France.

The boat was crammed with a large number of refugees of all nationalities, conditions were not good but it was better than the treatment that they would have received at the hands of the enemy. They reached Gibraltar without incident, being given a wonderful welcome with the town thrown open to them – everything was free, food, drink, theatres, cinemas, and hotel accommodation. They were scheduled originally only to stay in Gibraltar one night, however, Nat was recognized by some of the troops there and was persuaded to stay on for a number of impromptu concerts. In fact, the Servicemen were loath to let them go and in the end Nat and Stella had to be more or less smuggled out of the garrison.

It was just as well that they had the pleasant interlude in Gibraltar for the last stage of their journey back to England was anything but pleasant. Their transportation was a rather ancient coal boat and within a short space of time most of the passengers looked like refugees from the Black and White Minstrel Show. The small collier, jammed almost to the top of the funnel with six hundred and seventy passengers, took seven days to reach Liverpool. The passengers lived almost entirely on the deck; there was no soap, food and water were rationed, and the weather was terrible.

Conditions were so crowded, Nat had to sleep under a deck-gun that had been mounted to give some form of protection from enemy aircraft. At one point in the voyage he was woken by the noise of the gun being fired. On inquiring what the din was all about, he was informed by the gunner that an enemy submarine had passed beneath the boat. The sub decided to give chase. The old collier only did eight knots top speed normally but, somehow, the captain and his engineers managed to coax twelve knots out of her. The boat shook and shivered all over as the engines groaned under the strain, and every few minutes there was a rattle like machine-gun fire as the steering chains moved the rudder from side to side, zig-zagging. The sub fired two torpedoes but the wily old skipper of the coal boat was too clever for them and they missed their intended target. A great sigh of relief went up when the boat eventually steamed into Liverpool.

Back in England, Nat had to pick up the threads – all he knew was music. The outbreak of war terminated the so-successful Georgians combination that had delighted music fans all over the world for nearly five years. Things would never quite be the same again; they had been wonderful years. Pat Smuts looked back on that part in his life and likened it to being part of a big happy family, of which Nat was the head. Pat made no bones about the fact that Nat had been his inspiration and it would be difficult to find a better friend anywhere. Pat went on to do a good job in entertaining the troops during the war, and following it he joined the Skyrockets Orchestra, remaining with them for twelve years and having particularly happy memories of their run of shows at the London Palladium.

Jimmy Messini got together with Al Bowlly in the early part of 1940 to form a singing duo, billed as "The Radio Stars With Two Guitars" or "Two Voices And Guitars In Harmony", and they toured provincial variety theatres. Sadly, the act was not a great success, serving to emphasize the depths to which the once-acclaimed Al Bowlly had sunk in the public's favour. Rather ironically, many felt that at this stage in his career he was singing better than ever. Strangely enough, both Al Jolson and Bing Crosby had a few "off" years, but shortly before their deaths they were singing with a richness that only maturity can bring. In the case of

Al Bowlly, we were not destined to find out whether he would hit the big time again for he was killed in his flat during a bombing raid on London on 17 April, 1941. Such is the power of nostalgia, forty years after his death re-issues of his old recordings have made him a cult figure.

In 1940, despite the fact that musicians were being called up for the Services at a quite alarming rate, leaving many of the top bands struggling to maintain a line-up, Nat decided to form a new band, bigger than before. Billed as Nat Gonella and the New Georgians, the group comprised Jack Wallace and Cyril Oughton on trumpets, Miff King on trombone, Micky Seidman, Jack Bonsor, Jock Middleton and Joe Moore on saxes and clarinets, Will Hemmings on bass, Norman Stenfalt on piano, Johnny Roland on drums and Roy Dexter on guitar and vocals. And of course, vocals were also supplied by Stella Moya. The posters advertising the band's appearances were often headed "Mr. and Mrs. Swing", for Nat and Stella were married in the summer of 1940 at Hendon.

The New Georgians provided the type of music that most big bands in the early war years were playing, the sort of "Music While You Work" stuff that inspired factory workers and Servicemen alike, not forgetting the poor souls cowering in air-raid shelters and sleeping rough on the platforms of the Underground. The generation of today, reared on the works of Boy George, Bananarama, Duran Duran, and Echo And The Bunnymen, would no doubt scoff at numbers such as "I've Got Sixpence", "Hey Little Hen", "The Hut-Sut Song" and "Yes, My Darling Daughter", but this was the music that cheered the nation when it badly needed cheering. Nat and his New Georgians recorded all the above numbers for Columbia, and a lot more besides. The following titles may revive a few memories: "In The Mood", "At The Woodchopper's Ball", "I Got Rhythm", "Tuxedo Junction", "Beat Me Daddy, Eight To The Bar", "Aurora", and "I Haven't Time To Be A Millionaire". The vocal charms of Stella Moya were put to good use on songs such as "Jumpin' Jive", "Never Took A Lesson In My Life", and "Time On My Hands". While the rich voice of Roy Dexter scored with "If I Could Be With You One Hour Tonight", "You Came Along", "I

Understand", and "Mean To Me". On hearing the dulcet tones of Roy Dexter today on those records, one may reflect that he was perhaps one of the most underrated male singers of that period.

Through his natural gift of music, Nat did what he could to keep the morale of civilians and Service people high, especially for the latter. When called upon to entertain the troops, he always did his utmost to get to a concert, sometimes travelling long distances under bad conditions. There was one particular troop show that stood out in his mind. It took place not too far from where he was living at the time, Edgware, London. Although he had two cars, a Hudson Terraplane and an Opel Shooting Brake, he used a motor-cycle for short distances in order to eke out his petrol ration. The machine was really more like a moped and after he had done his solo turn at an Army camp, a sergeant offered him a lift home on a truck. Nat explained that he had his bike with him but the sergeant said: "That's all right, we can put it in the back of the truck." Nat sat up front in the cabin with the sergeant and a driver. They had travelled but a few miles when someone remarked: "Can you smell burning?" Looking behind them, they discovered to their horror that the rear of the truck was ablaze. Evidently, petrol had trickled out of the tank of Nat's bike, and had somehow caught alight. Rushing to the back of the vehicle, they pulled the motor-cycle off. Nat checked it over, it appeared to be perfectly intact, so he rode off, leaving the soldiers still trying to put out the fire.

In July 1941, Nat made a record with Johnny Claes and the Claepigions, "Stompin' At The Savoy" and "How Am I To Know". Claes was a young Belgian trumpeter who had come to Nat before the war for lessons; he was also an ardent racing driver. The line-up for the record included Ivor Mairants, ex-Roy Fox, Ambrose and Geraldo guitarist, and the vocal for "How Am I To Know" was provided by a young Benny Lee.

During that same month the New Georgians began a five-week engagement at Green's famous Playhouse Ballroom in Glasgow, the best band-date in the British Isles at that time. It was while they were playing at this prodigious venue that the bombshell dropped. Nat received his calling-up papers. Things were difficult enough, there were only two of the original band left from the outfit of the previous year, but to lose the leader of the band could spell only disaster.

In his showbiz column in the *Evening News*, critic Jack Robertson strongly highlighted the futility of putting people such as Nat Gonella into uniform, stating that he would be better employed maintaining the spirits of the masses than digging trenches in the Pioneer Corps. Robertson also suggested that the £25 a week Nat Gonella was paying in Income Tax towards funds for the war was another good argument in favour of exemption. He also pointed out that Nat already was doing a good job for the war effort by parading his band gratuitously for troops and factory workers. What did Nat himself think about his call-up? Philosophically he said: "Well, if I have to go, it's nice to think that it is from Green's, the best play-date in the country."

In his column, Robertson also revealed that Nat's wife and vocalist, Stella Moya, might have a go at carrying on the Gonella outfit when Nat left to go into the Forces. A few weeks later the *Evening News* gossip column had a short piece on Stella, describing her as one of the few women to lead a top-line West End band in London. The band was then playing at the Empress in Brixton.

Nat's version of his interview for the Services reads more like a comedy script. Officer: "What are you?" Nat: "I'm a musician." Officer: "Any trade?" Nat: "No." Officer: "Well, you are not much good to the Army." Nat: "No." Officer: "What's your name?" Nat: "Gonella." Officer: "Ah, I see, Italian eh?" With that he designated Britain's best-known trumpeter to the Pioneer Corps with all the foreigners and illiterates.

As Private Gonella, Nat's income dropped from something in the region of £150 a week to 17s. 6d. a week gross, 10s. net. Still, we have no reason to believe that he dug too many of those trenches, the only thing in life that he really dug was music. In October 1941 he was to be found leading a small band of khaki musicians at Belle Vue Barracks. In a short time, the group had gained a fair reputation by playing at troop shows, regimental dances, and occasional charity concerts.

Towards the end of 1941, a group was formed by Lieutenant Basil Brown with a view to providing entertainment for military establishments in remote areas. Former professional entertainers, now in khaki, were drawn from units all over Britain. Officially known as the Central Pool of Artistes, this unit developed into the renowned "Stars in Battledress".

Nat Gonella was selected to be one of the first "Stars in Battledress", and duly reported to the Royal Ordnance Depot at Greenford in Middlesex. He was in good company, rubbing shoulders with Charlie Chester, George Melachrino, and Boy Foy, among others. They had to parade for inspection every morning with the rest of the depot, following which the entertainment unit members retired to a Nissen structure known as Hut 13 for rehearsals. They were a pretty motley bunch on parade, in fact their general turn-out was guaranteed to make most Regular Army N.C.O.s weep. Nat never really took the Army seriously and it was quite an event to see him wearing boots; he even went on parade in brown suede shoes. Neither was his punctuality all that it might have been, although it was noticeable that the parades never started until Nat had arrived, usually making a grand entrance in a car, rather reminiscent of the days when he drove into town to meet his fans.

Of course, one thing that he did take seriously was his music, whether he was playing to troops in a canteen, village hall, on the back of a lorry or from an improvised stage in the middle of a field, he always performed as if he was at the Palladium. In addition to live appearances, he was also involved in recording special radio shows for the War Office which were later relayed to British troops serving overseas. This venture was handled by Second Lieut. George Black, son of the West End impresario, assisted by Lance Corporal Michael Carr. Carr was a songwriter in Civvy Street, having penned "South Of The Border". Sid Millward, of Nitwits fame, was also involved in the recordings.

Meanwhile, Stella was still battling to keep the vastly-depleted Georgians on the road. Sometimes Nat was able to put in an appearance, usually for Sunday concerts. Patrick Griffiths, a life-long Gonella fan, still has fond memories of one of those Sunday shows that he saw at the Colston Hall in Bristol in 1942. For Patrick it was sheer magic as Nat and the band swung their way through at least twenty numbers, from "Georgia On My Mind" to "Beat Me Daddy, Eight To The Bar". Now living in Warminster, Wiltshire, Pat still cherishes the programmes and the autographed photos he has of Nat, Stella, and the Georgians. From those programmes it would seem that West Country music fans were well catered for at the Colston Hall in 1942, with appearances by Carroll Gibbons, Jay Wilbur and Harry Roy. At that time, Harry Roy was featuring his "Come And Lead The Band" novelty item in his bandshow, this was when members of the audience were invited to try their hand at conducting the band, the best baton-waver of the heat going forward to the grand final on Saturday night. This was great for the box-office, with friends and relatives of the finalists flocking to the theatre to give support.

Back to military matters. Although he was not entirely happy in uniform, Nat was surviving his service in the Forces reasonably well. Then, he was dealt another body blow by his superiors, he was posted overseas. In the cause of secrecy, as with most wartime postings, he was not informed where he was being sent. Three weeks later, following a train ride to Scotland and an uncomfortable trip on a troopship, he found himself in North Africa.

Stuck in the desert at a waterhole called Philipville, Nat was not a happy man. He hated being in the Army, and in particular he hated being in the Pioneer Corps, for it was accepted that they fell for every rotten job under the sun. Then, fate played another hand. The band of the Royal Tank Regiment were camped some twenty miles away, they were about to give a concert and on hearing that Nat Gonella was in the vicinity, they invited him along as a guest artist. On his part, Nat was only too happy to stop digging ablutions, or whatever the Pioneer Corps did, for a few hours. The concert went well, everyone was happy. Nat was even happier for he never went back to the Pioneer Corps, as a transfer to the Tank Regiment was arranged for him immediately.

Nat travelled with the Tank Regiment band all over North Africa and into Sicily and Italy. In the early days of September, 1943, the

*Private Gonella, star in battledress.* (Gonella Collection)

*Bruts Gonella has a problem with currency on the Georgians tour of Holland in 1945. Monty Montgomery is in the background.* (Gonella Collection)

Allied Forces crossed the Straits of Messina. As they were about to set forth for the fray ahead, a company of Canadian soldiers was entertained by Nat and the regimental band in the middle of a field, surrounded by tents, wagons, and armoured vehicles. It was a marvellous night, good music, a raucous singsong, and plenty of vino. The following morning the Canadian troops moved out to do battle and as each truck left the camp Nat stood by the gate blowing them a farewell on his trumpet. It was a particularly poignant moment and one that Nat would never forget. He played an individual farewell to at least thirty-five truckloads of soldiers. Sadly, he never saw or heard from any of those guys again.

There was another incident around that time that had happier associations, when he received an unexpected visitor. Camped near Naples, he was resting in his tent one afternoon, having a pleasant little doze, when suddenly he was brought back to reality by a voice yelling in his ear: "Right Gonella, on your feet there, get fell-in outside!" Nat shot out of his bunk like a bullet from a gun. As his senses began to return, he recognized the face behind the voice. It was Eddie Carroll, his pianist pal from the Lew Stone days. Eddie, who was a staff sergeant in the R.A.O.C., learned that Nat was in the camp so with the help of another sergeant he played this jolly little jape on his old friend. As one may imagine, Nat's immediate reaction was quite colourful, however, it was not long before he and Eddie were chatting over old times.

Although Nat did not know about it at the time, his voice and trumpet were providing an important service for an Army camp somewhere in the desert. Arthur Roberts, an old soldier and desert campaigner, has a particular memory of a camp he was stationed at in 1944 in a desert outpost near Murzmatru. The only entertainment available for the soldiers camped there was a cinema some four miles away. The big problem was the walk back to the camp when the film show had finished, for when darkness falls in the desert, it really falls. Pitch black. A corporal at the camp, who also happened to be an ardent Gonella fan, solved the problem for his buddies by playing a record over the loudspeakers of the public address system. Corporal Nat, as he became known, would play the same record every night, Nat Gonella singing "Stardust". Just imagine this scene, a group of Army lads are groping their way back to the camp when suddenly the sound of a golden trumpet is heard drifting across the desert, followed by a distinctive voice singing "Sometimes I wonder why I spent the lonely night, just dreaming of a song, the melody haunts my revelry, and I am once again with you". It really was music to their ears; they headed in the direction from which it was coming, and before long they were back in the safety of their tents.

Following their morale-boosting efforts in the Italian Campaign, the band of the Royal Tank Regiment were ordered back to England, thus giving Nat the opportunity to shake some of the sand out of his boots and out of his trumpet. He was given two weeks' leave, during which his stomach began playing him up, and he was forced to report sick. A specialist confirmed that Nat had a duodenal ulcer, which resulted in the military authorities making the momentous decision to dispense with his services. Nat handed back his uniform only days before the Tank Regiment band left for France following the first invasion landings.

In civilian clothes once again, he had time to ponder on his situation. The war had demolished his great American Dream, his Army service had cost him something in the region of £16,000 through loss of earnings, and, to top it all, Stella had left him. Evidently she preferred the company of an American Air Force colonel. Yes, as far as Nat was concerned, Adolf Hitler had a lot to answer for.

*The New Georgians. 1941.* (Patrick Griffiths Collection)

# 9

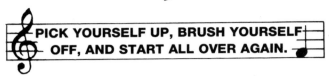

Despite his financial losses, Nat had managed to save a bit, and set about spending it with great gusto. In his own words: "I suppose I was something of a playboy then, nightclubs, race meetings, birds and booze, you name it. To me it was easy come, easy go."

Eventually, someone suggested that he got a band together. He had got the playboy bit out of his system by then, so, no doubt influenced by his dwindling bank-balance, he did indeed form a band. Under the auspices of Jack Hylton, he took it to Holland only a few weeks after the war had ended. This pleased Nat considerably for he had been one of the last musicians to leave Holland at the outbreak of war, and here he was again, one of the first back.

His new outfit was in the big-band image and is described by Nat as follows: "The band had about thirteen pieces, there was five brass and I used to do the Harry James thing then, sing a few blues, and blow my brains out over the top of the brass section." The band personnel included Bruts Gonella, Monty Montgomery, and Fred Dinning on trumpets, Frank Osborne on trombone, Jock Forbes, Ken Lumb, Dennis Cracknell and Chris Curtis on saxes and clarinets, Eddie Farrow on piano, Bill Haines on bass, and Phil Seamen on drums. Vocals were taken care of by Helen Mack.

It was good to have his brother Bruts back in the line-up. Bruts had also had some interesting experiences during the war while serving in the Marines. It may seem strange that Bruts should be put in the Marines for he was even shorter than Nat but, of course, he was in the band section of this Service. He managed to keep blowing his beloved horn, although his career almost came to a sudden end in 1942 when the ship that he was in, H.M.S. *Glasgow*, was hit by an enemy torpedo. However, this incident had a happy ending for Bruts, as the ship limped into New York Harbour for a refit and they remained there for six months. Because he was in uniform, he was allowed into clubs, theatres and shows free. One night he went to see Tommy Dorsey and his orchestra, and during the interval he popped around backstage and introduced himself as Nat Gonella's brother. After he had a drink and a chat with the boys in the band, seeing that he had his mouthpiece with him, they invited Bruts to have a blow with them on the bandstand. This was an opportunity that he was unlikely to refuse, and duly obliged with "I Can't Give You Anything But Love, Baby". Incidentally that same night saw the debut of a skinny and awfully nervous young singer, Frank Sinatra. During his New York sojourn Bruts also had a memorable session with Benny Goodman in which he played "I Found A New Baby".

The post-war Georgians did not record so prolifically as the earlier groups, only producing about eight sides on the Decca label,

*Helen Mack, lovely vocalist with the New Georgians.*   *Nat with his third wife Dorothy. She won his heart with new-laid eggs.* (Gonella Collection)

mostly hits of the day such as "One Meat Ball", "Let Him Go, Let Him Tarry", "Put The Blame On Mame" and "Shoo-Fly Pie And Apple Pan Dowdy". Although these numbers got the most airing, the side that appealed most to those with jazz leanings was "Gnat Jump", written by Nat himself. He also cut "Put The Blame On Mame" on a later disc he did in 1947 when he went to Sweden to play again with the Thore Ehrling Orchestra, the reverse side being "Five Minutes More". This proved to be his last recording session for ten years.

Trumpeter Monty Montgomery fondly recalled this period with the Georgians: "Phil Seamen and I worked for Nat and he was the greatest, the best. About once a week he would sack Phil and myself, for cheek or something, then the next day he'd take us back again. That sound of his, enormous! We played Green's in Glasgow; posters advertising Nat Gonella and his Georgians were everywhere and there would be six thousand people dancing on the floor. It was so packed the notes would just fall out of the instrument on to the floor. But you could go right to the back of the hall and still hear Nat like a bell. Yes, a marvellous man to work for, and a magnificent jazz musician."

Glamorous singer Helen Mack is also full of praise for Nat as a boss. She recalled one particular gig when the band were playing in Rhyl, the piano player failed to turn up for some reason or another. Although she was no great shakes on the piano, Helen offered to fill in for him. She described her playing as "lousy", drawing black looks from the rest of the band whenever she played a bum note. However, at the end of the week she found that Nat had given her some extra money in her wages, it was his way of showing his appreciation for her willingness to help out.

Helen Mack also played a part in a meeting that was to affect Nat's life considerably. He had been through a six-year period that had provided more downs than ups, then in May 1946 something went right for him, he met his third wife, Dorothy. When they first met at the Court Royal Hotel in Southampton, Dorothy formed the opinion that he was rather grumpy and was not all that impressed. She said as much to Helen, who had introduced them in the first place. Then Helen revealed that Nat was having a bad time with stomach ulcers. Dorothy felt so sorry for him she made a special trip into the New Forest to find a farm, returning with a carton of new laid eggs. In 1946, this was indeed a luxury. Romance blossomed and it was a case of third time lucky for Nat, for he and Dorothy have been together for nearly forty years. So he had solved his personal problems but many years of fluctuating fortunes lay ahead in his career as a musician.

Musical tastes were changing, the Georgians thirteen-piece band gradually fell to ten, then eight, and eventually to a quartet. Nat even tried a comedy band, still billed as Nat Gonella's Georgians, but it was not a great success. Not being one to give up easily, he went modern and formed a bebop band, one of the first of its kind in this country. But, it was not really Nat's scene and although he persevered with it for some time, Dorothy Gonella probably summed it up best when she described it as "gas-oven music". The bop band comprised Phil Seamen, Lennie Bush, Johnny Rogers, Roy Plummer and Kenny Graham.

Travelling around the country with his bebop band reminded Nat of his early Georgian days in the mid-Thirties. The manager of a hall would remark: "What is that noise that you are playing?" Nat would reply: "It's swing, it's the new music." It was the same with bebop. "What is that noise that you are playing?" – "It's bebop, it's the new music." Only this time the managers would reply: "Well, take it away, and don't bring it back." In the end, the music even got through to Nat himself, it shattered his nerves and he went to bed every night with a blinding headache. He eventually disbanded the bebop outfit while he still had his sanity.

One of Nat Gonella's biggest setbacks in the post-war years was his rejection by the B.B.C. The corporation was undergoing a shake-up at the time with an Australian ex-band leader named Jim Davidson put in charge of the dance music side of the Variety Department. When Nat applied for broadcasts he was informed brusquely that he would have to give an audition like everyone else. Davidson made it obvious that he had never heard of Nat Gonella. He told Nat that he was looking for someone like Harry James and

Nat politely informed him that he did not have to copy Harry James, he was Nat Gonella and he had his own style. It was to no avail, he still had to do the audition. Getting together a scratch band to back his vocals and trumpet, he appeared before Davidson and a panel of six producers. It was more like the Inquisition. "Thank you, we will let you know." After regularly broadcasting over the airwaves for more than twenty years, he had failed the audition.

Another audition that Nat would have liked to have forgotten took place in Brighton. He was hanging around Archer Street one day, at a loose end, when he bumped into his former bass player and vocalist from the wartime New Georgians, Roy Dexter. It transpired that Roy was in a predicament: he had a duo act with another musician who played the trumpet but, unfortunately, his partner had dropped dead on the stage just before an important audition. Nat had nothing on so he offered to team up with Roy for a spell to help him out. The audition was at Butlin's holiday hotel near Brighton and the intrepid duo turned up in the hope of better things to follow. One of the big numbers in the act was "Big Noise From Winnetka", in which Roy played the bass while Nat beat hell out of the strings of the instrument with a couple of drumsticks, as per Bob Crosby's Bobcats. Nat was a trumpeter, not a drummer, although he did have some experience of beating the skins from his early days at St. Mary's. Anyhow, he did his darndest at the audition, bashing those bass strings until the veins stood out on his forehead and his arms felt like they were about to fall off. His labours were in vain, they failed the Butlin's audition. It turned out that one of the members of the audition panel had also been on the B.B.C. panel.

Putting their Brighton experience behind them, Gonella and Dexter managed to get booked by the Hal Monty organization. Hal Monty was a comedian on the halls and ran a theatrical agency. Hal had a contract to provide entertainment for American Servicemen stationed on the Continent so the musical pair found themselves trundling bass and trumpet in the direction of Paris. On arrival, they booked into a Number Three hotel, it was not the Ritz but it was clean and somewhere to put their heads down between shows.

The next day they made themselves known to Ted Easton, who

was the entertainments officer for all the U.S. forces in France, and the man who had their schedule worked out for them. They travelled to the first show in Ted's shining new automobile but he was not too happy about Roy's great bass fiddle being transported in his new car, so from thereon alternative means of travel were arranged. They were due to do the act at an American base some distance from Paris and they opted to negotiate the journey by train. Arriving at the station, they tried to board the waiting train but a porter would not let them get on with Roy's bass. He could not speak English, they could not speak French, and while they were arguing and gesticulating, the train moved out. Nat and Roy hurried back to the hotel just in time to catch Ted Easton. After scanning a railway timetable, Ted found that there was an express train leaving shortly that would get them to their destination in time for the show. Back at the station, Ted kept the porter occupied while Nat and Roy bulldozed their way with the bass on to the train. The porter was still arguing as the train was moving.

Ted Easton had made the arrangements for them to be met at the other end and they were duly whisked away at top speed to the camp where they were to provide their entertainment. It was only after they had arrived that they discovered that Hal Monty had sold them as a fifty-minute act. They had a slight problem, their act lasted only fifteen minutes. Luckily, Nat had plenty of numbers up his sleeve, and somehow they managed to pad it out for fifty minutes.

Their French tour of the American bases lasted ten days. It could not exactly be described as a rip-roaring success and following the B.B.C. and Butlin's audition failures, it left Nat feeling pretty low. In later years he would be able to look back and laugh about those days when he and Roy Dexter trundled that great bass around Paris but at the time it was anything but funny. Really, the only good thing to come out of the French trip was his introduction to Ted Easton, a factor that would become apparent later.

Nat and Roy spent the summer season of 1949 at Sandown in the Isle of Wight, playing on the pier and at the Sandringham Hotel with Les Jessop on drums. After touring the clubs in the winter period, Nat went out on his own in the summer of 1950 for a season at the Coronation Holiday Camp at Hayling Island. He was the camp's musical director and could be found blowing most nights in Ye Olde Barn, accompanied by pianists Roy or Eddie Harris, and Stan Howell or Glen Haywood on drums. In the Coronation Ballroom he played opposite the Johnny Lyne Band from Portsmouth. Johnny Lyne was a great clarinet player, his talent being recognized in 1953 when he was given the Melody Maker Award for that year. Nat also played concerts every Sunday with a nine-piece band, and on Thursdays he played with the Stan Matthews Quartet, another Portsmouth group. So, one way and another, Nat and Dorothy, not forgetting their Alsatian dog Georgia (all their dogs were named Georgia), had a pleasant season at Hayling Island.

*Nat and Dorothy with Georgia their Alsation at Coronation Holiday Camp at Hayling Island, 1950. (Courtesy of Chris Hayes)*

*Nat with a young admirer at the Coronation Holiday Camp. (Courtesy of Chris Hayes)*

When the Hayling season finished in September, Nat went to Southampton for the opening of a restaurant club attached to the Palm Court Sports Stadium, and stayed on as musical director with a five-piece band. The sporting club operated greyhound racing and speedway racing and there are at least two tales relating to Nat with these sports. The first concerns the night he was taken around the speedway track on the back of a motor-bike. As the bike sped around the bends at 35 m.p.h., there was Nat clinging on with one hand and playing his trumpet with the other, almost choking as cinders were thrown up into the bell of the instrument. The other tale is associated with dog racing. For someone with Nat's gambling instincts, it was not the ideal place to work. The story goes that while he was performing on the bandstand in the club, he held his trumpet in such a way that he could make pre-arranged signals with his fingers through the large observation window to a friend outside, who subsequently placed bets for him on the dogs.

In the early 1950s, Nat returned to his old love, the variety stage, touring with the Cheeky Chappie himself, the one and only Max Miller. Max had acquired a reputation for being difficult to work with but Nat got on with him very well, his Cockney accent no doubt proving the perfect foil for the Miller brand of humour. Max was also a wonderful golfer, very shrewd and cunning, and with Nat as his partner they played a number of interesting foursomes. It is reasonable to assume that many of their opponents formed the opinion that Max Miller made more money on the golf course than the stage. Max's famous saying was "Now, there's a funny thing", originating from his equally famous gag: "Now, 'ere's a funny thing. I went home to the wife last night. Now, that is a funny thing!" There is a nice little story concerning the night that Max was playing at the old Theatre Royal in Portsmouth: after finishing his act he rushed out of the theatre and sped in the direction of the railway station in order to catch the last train. Puffing up the steps to the platform, he reached it just in time to see the train steaming out of the station. A porter standing by the staircase turned to Max and said with a grin: "Now, there's a funny thing." Max's reply was unprintable.

In addition to Nat, the Max Miller Show had a number of good supporting acts, including Alfred Thripp the blind pianist, Margaret and Billy West, Clarkson and Leslie, and glamour on the high wire in the shapely form of Georgette. Although Nat and Max had plenty of laughs during the tour, it was all really rather sad, for they were taking part in the death throes of British variety. It became a

Nat with Max Miller during their tour of the halls in the 1950's. (Gonella Collection)

Nat and Dorothy with Max Miller at Great Yarmouth. (Gonella Collection)

standing joke that they closed more theatres than anyone else in the profession, with almost every Max Miller Show poster having a white strip plastered across it announcing: "CLOSING – LAST WEEK". Revered bastions of entertainment such as the Shepherd's Bush Empire, Hackney Empire, Wood Green Empire, Finsbury Park Empire, New Cross Empire, Woolwich Empire, and the Golders Green Hippodrome were closed to variety addicts in London alone, destined to become television studios, supermarkets, or piles of brick rubble. Smaller theatres such as the Collins Music Hall on Islington Green or the Bedford Theatre in Camden Town hung on for a while with shows called "Nudes Of The World" or "Strip, Strip, Hooray!", vehicles that allowed demure ladies such as Phyllis Dixey, Jane of the *Daily Mirror*, Rosemarie Andree, and Ramena the Coloured Nude to display their obvious charms.

A radio spot did eventually come Nat's way via the Leon Cortez Show. Cortez will be remembered for his Cockney Professor routine with his wife, Doreen Harris, acting as his stooge and supplying the occasional song. Being a Cockney, Nat blended into the show nicely, and it was great fun. Before he went into his weekly solo musical spot, there would always be a bit of light-hearted banter with Leon and Doreen in front of the mike. Leon would introduce him with lines such as: "And now mates, it has been said as how Nat Gonella is the finest trumpet player in the world. Now, here is the man who said it, Nat Gonella!" Doreen comes on with a telegram for Nat from a listener. Nat reads it out loud: "Dear Mister Gonella, when you sing, your voice swells to High Heaven." Cortez grabs the telegram. "That's not swells, it's smells!" Nat would then launch into his solo accompanied by a large studio orchestra and a vocal group, playing showmanship pieces such as "St. Louis Blues" or "Ciribiribin".

The shows that Nat did with Max Miller and Leon Cortez were definitely morale boosters for him. However, there was one with band leader Ted Heath that was an absolute disaster. It came about when a consortium fronted by Ted Heath were buying up shares in the decaying Selmer music empire for a project that they had planned. Nat had been formerly associated with Selmer's and both

*Getting hep with Professor Leon Cortez and singer Doreen Harris in the early 50s.*
(Courtesy of Chris Hayes)

he and Louis Armstrong were featured at various times by the firm for advertising trumpets. He also had 2,000 shares in Selmer's that he had bought for around 2s. a share. It transpired that Nat was holding up the transactions by hanging on to his shares but he was not all that bothered about selling them. In the end, he agreed to sell the shares to Heath, part of the deal being that he would be given a solo spot on one of Heath's prestigious Sunday bandshows at the London Palladium. Although he sold the shares for twice as much as he paid for them, Nat's main objective was to use the show as a means of getting back into the limelight.

The big day arrived, the Palladium was packed to the roof. Ted Heath was riding high at the time, and his big band numbers such as "Hot Toddy" meant good business in the record shops. He also had a formidable line up of vocalists in the form of Lita Roza, Denis Lotis and Dickie Valentine. Nat was waiting in the wings while Dickie Valentine did his singing spot, which included impressions of singing stars. It was intended that he should finish with his Mario Lanza take-off but the shouts for an encore encouraged him to go into his Johnnie Ray impersonation with "Cry". After he had acknowledged the applause, instead of introducing Nat there and then, Valentine announced: "Thank you ladies and gentlemen, that was my impression of Johnnie 'Cry' Ray, but I am pleased to say that we have the man himself here tonight in the audience". A spotlight swept to a box at the side of the theatre. Pandemonium broke out, the audience went wild, screaming, swooning, and running up and down the aisles shouting "Johnnie!" at their idol in his box. Amid all this commotion, it was almost impossible to hear the voice of Dickie Valentine: "And now ladies and gentlemen, Nat Gonella!"

Nat strolled onto the great stage to the sounds of "Georgia On My Mind". He need not have bothered, as far as the audience were concerned, he was not even in the building. He was too good a trouper to give in, he blew and he blew, the more they ignored him the more determined he became to get over to them. And while he was fighting the good fight, there was Johnnie Ray up in his box doing his royal wave and blowing kisses to the hordes of young girls below. He had all the attention, and he hadn't sung a note.

As Nat finished his first number, there was not even a ripple of applause, nothing. He went into his second song but it was hopeless, and in the end he walked off the stage in despair. That this should happen to him at the London Palladium of all places, on the same stage from which he had received his fair share of adulation in better days. There is an addendum to this story which highlights the fickle moods of music fans. On a tour of Britain in 1984, Johnnie Ray gave a concert at the Portsmouth Guildhall. There was not even enough people in the audience to fill the first two rows, so the pendulum swings.

Nat was frustrated several times in the 1950s when it came to television appearances, there was a lot of talk but, for one reason or another, nothing came of it. Could it have been Billy Cotton's influence? We shall never know. Having said that, Nat did make a rare television appearance in the Max Wall Show in 1955. He and Max did a duet, "I'll See You In My Dreams", with Max playing the trombone.

Nat fooling around with David          Two old friends "Chew the Fat". Louis
Hughes, Joe "Piano" Henderson, and     Armstrong's message on this photo
John Slater during a break from a      gave Nat the will to carry on when
variety tour at the Nottingham Empire. things were going badly for him in the
(Gonella Collection)                   late 1950s. (Gonella Collection)

Things got steadily worse. Where he had once earned hundreds of
pounds, he was glad to get a few pounds in the hope of keeping the
wolf from the door. He was forced to play in seedy clubs and pubs,
sharing dressing rooms with strippers and blue comedians. Sometimes he would travel miles to find a remote pub way out in the
country, where he was expected to do his act in a bar smaller than
many people's living rooms. In one particularly tough club on the
Northern circuit, he went on for his first spot and was waiting to do
a second later in the evening when he was approached by the club
secretary. This cloth-capped gent informed Nat that he would not
be required to do a second spot, and paid him off with £10, plus a
farewell delivered with typical Northern bluntness: "Ay, and we've
got better bloody bugle-players in't' Town Band!"

In the late 1950s, Nat and Dorothy were living in Southampton,
in the suburb of Bitterne. Their situation looked awfully bleak,
although the trad boom was sweeping the country and jazz musicians such as Kenny Ball, Acker Bilk and Chris Barber were

receiving the adulation of millions, nobody wanted to know Nat Gonella. A friend offered him a part-time job in a bookmaker's office. Nat took it.

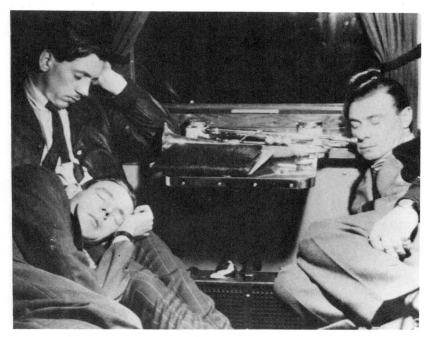

*"Letting The Train Take The Strain". Just as a cowboy sleeps with his horse, Nat sleeps with his trumpet.* (Gonella Collection)

# 10

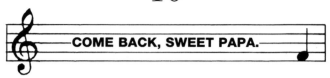

**COME BACK, SWEET PAPA.**

When music has been your life for nearly forty years, it is difficult to turn your back on it. For Nat Gonella, it was impossible. Whether he was playing for £100 a night, or £10, whether he was performing for two thousand people, or twenty, blowing that horn was in his blood. He just had to make a come-back.

In March, 1959, Nat found himself sitting in a dressing room in a tiny theatre at Herne Bay, Kent. He knew that when he strode out through that dressing room door to the stage beyond, he was taking his first steps on the long road back. On the table in front of him lay a telegram wishing him good luck, it was from his old friend Louis Armstrong. He also had a photograph of Louis and himself, sent by his idol. A message was scrawled across the picture: TO NAT, WHO I STILL THINK AFTER ALL THESE YEARS IS A GREAT MUSICIAN AND ONE OF THE GREATEST HUMAN BEING'S THAT I HAVE MET IN MY WHOLE LIFE. GOD BLESS YOU NAT, AND CARRY ON WITH THAT HORN, WE HAVE TO STAY AROUND TO KEEP THESE YOUNGSTERS HAPPY. KEEP PLAYING THAT MUSIC FROM THE HEART. With encouragement like that, from the master himself, Nat had to keep trying. He went out on to that small stage in Herne Bay and blew as if he was on the stage of the Palladium. Gonella was back.

In the summer of 1959, Nat took a five-piece band to Jersey for the season. Before catching the boat, they played a gig at a club in his home base of Southampton. Then they boarded the overnight boat for the Channel Islands, eventually reaching Jersey. Their residency was in the luxurious Rainbow Room on the island, and they had to be pretty versatile, providing music for dancing and cabaret. The cabaret acts were mixed, varying from pop singers to a troupe of Russian acrobats, and Nat and the band had to supply the supporting music for them. With his experience of many years on the variety stage, this did not bother Nat too much but the rest of the band had done nothing like it before. Anyhow, after a couple of rehearsals they managed to produce a passable sound.

It was while he was playing in Jersey that Nat was plagued temporarily by something that he had not experienced before in his musical career, his lip went – completely paralysed. He could not afford to give up at that stage so he had to carry on playing somehow. He was forced to lower his range and, although he knew that he was not blowing the horn to his usual high standard, he managed to busk his way through the rest of the engagement.

As the season in Jersey progressed, Nat found that he was receiving an increasing number of requests to play jazz numbers so he included a few jazz pieces in their cabaret act, such as "St. Louis Blues" and "Basin Street Blues". This went down very well with the holidaymakers, so they built up their repertoire of jazz standards, thus rekindling Nat's interest in the music. When he returned to Southampton at the end of the season, he formed a small jazz band and played around the South Coast.

Word got around about the great jazz that was being played throughout the summer in Jersey and around the Southampton area, resulting in the Lyn Dutton Agency getting in touch with Nat. The Dutton agency handled musicians such as Humphrey Lyttelton, Acker Bilk, Alex Welsh and Kenny Ball. Under its guidance, Nat's fortunes rapidly improved, helped by an L.P. produced by recording executive Denis Preston for Columbia. Called "Salute to Satchmo", the record included such gems as "Mack The Knife", "When It's Sleepy Time Down South", and "Georgia On My Mind". It was praised by the Press, receiving plaudits from the most hardened music critics. Charles Fox in the *Evening Standard* wrote: British jazz has certainly leapt ahead since the days when Nat Gonella was leading his Georgians, but that does not make Nat a has-been! This L.P. shows that he has lost neither his lip or his enthusiasm, and his tone seems warmer and more sensitive than it used to be. Dazzling Nat! More please!" Writing in the *Tatler*, the Hon. Gerald Lascelles had this to say: "This happy-go-lucky record contains some of the most listenable jazz that I have heard from a recording studio in England."

Encouraged by reports such as this, Nat formed a six-piece band that could boast the talents of some of the best jazz musicians on the British scene at that time. Called Nat Gonella And His Georgia Jazz Band, the group had Teddy Layton on clarinet, Bobby Mickleburgh on trombone, Lennie Felix on piano, Lennie Hastings on drums, and Alan Duddington on bass. The band made their debut on 6 February, 1960, at the Cavern Club in Liverpool, where it all began for the Beatles. The trad revival of the 1950s may have passed him by but this was Nat's great opportunity to get back into the big time and he was determined to make the most of it. The Cavern engagement was a great success, with over five hundred teenagers giving the Georgia Jazz Band a wildly enthusiastic reception. It was a marvellous occasion, and it moved Nat to exclaim: "Oh man, it's great to be back." The Press agreed, with several critics proclaiming that Nat Gonella could still show the younger jazzmen a thing or two when it came to technique, swing, and ideas.

Although the band included standard trad numbers in their programme – "Maryland", "Didn't He Ramble", "That's A Plenty", or "St. Louis Blues" – Nat refused to use a banjo player in the line-up. This was at a time when most trad bands looked naked without a banjo. However, a year or so later he did bring in a banjo player and admitted that he came to like it; it helped to swing the band along. At that time, Acker Bilk was the darling of the fans, and it was quite customary for the Georgia Jazz Band to be bombarded with requests from the audience to play "Summer-Set", Acker's big Top Twenty hit. Nat would usually reply: "I'm sorry folks, Acker has asked us not to play it for a week or two."

Nat and the Georgia Jazz Band played with Acker Bilk and his Paramount Jazz Band in a prestigious concert at the Royal Festival Hall in London. The hall was packed with Bilk fans who were ready to enthusiastically applaud everything and anything that their idol played. Despite this, Nat and the band went on and knocked them cold with "Mack The Knife" and "Show Me The Way To Go Home", receiving a tremendous ovation. One music critic was prompted to head his column: "Too much Acker, not enough Nat!"

Nat and the band had a very enjoyable tour with Acker Bilk and his band in the 1960s, taking in Sweden and Germany. There was one particular night in Hamburg that Nat would not forget in a hurry, most of the members of the two bands went out on the razzle to a nearby beer-garden but Nat and Acker were feeling rather tired so they stayed in their hotel rooms to rest. However, they soon recovered and decided to go out and join the boys for a beer or two. A small German band were playing at the gardens so it was really quite pleasant.

The word soon spread that Nat Gonella was there, which resulted in the German bandmaster coming over to Nat's table, followed by him marching Nat to the stand, thrusting a baton into his hand and inviting him to lead the band. Nat took up the challenge, in fact he did rather well and it was all jolly good fun. When they had finished the number, the bandmaster escorted Nat back to the table in order to knock back two glasses of beer that had been set up. The German musician emptied his glass with almost one gulp and when Nat had finished his, he was marched back to the bandstand and invited to act as conductor once again. When it was over they went through the same routine, back to the table, two glasses of beer, with the German downing his before Nat had hardly got the glass to his lips. Then, to the delight of everyone present they performed this ritual yet again. By this time, thanks to the strong German ale the band were beginning to sound more like fugitives from "Doctor Crock and his Crackpots". However, when Nat finally took his seat he sobered up very quickly, a buxom waitress presented him with a bill that worked out to about £10. It transpired that he had taken part in a form of contest, for the last person to finish their glass of beer had to pay for that round. No wonder his newly-acquired German friend had knocked back his drink so rapidly.

On 22 February, 1960, Nat had a request to report to a theatre to discuss a television show. When he arrived, he recognized a few

*Two of Britain's greatest exponents of the trumpet, Humphrey Lyttelton and Nat, pose for the camera.* (Gonella Collection)

familiar faces, and started chatting away. Suddenly, he was confronted by a large man with an Irish accent holding a book in his hands. "Nat Gonella, jazz pioneer and hero of a real life stage romance, this is your life!" Eamonn Andrews. Nat couldn't believe it. "No, you must be kidding. I couldn't fall for that." But he had, the doors of the theatre opened and the audience came flooding in. As Nat was led away by the conspirators to get ready for the programme, if one listened closely it was possible to hear "You sods".

The show began in earnest, with Nat alternatively sitting down and standing up in order to greet old friends as they were introduced to the nation via the television screen. The guests included George Latimer, his boyhood pal from St. Mary's, trumpeter Fred Wood from the Busby Boys, saxophonist Pat Smuts from the original Georgians, pianist Eddie Carroll, his old boss Lew Stone, and Jack Turland, the blind trumpeter whom Nat had helped in Birmingham before the war.

*"Nat Gonella – This Is Your Life"* 22–2–60. *l to r: Eddie Carroll, Pat Smuts, Alan Duddington, Helen Mack, Lennie Hastings, Nat, Teddy Layton, Dorothy, Humphrey Lyttelton, Jack Turland, Fred Wood, Bobby Mickleburgh, Lew Stone, Eddie Rogers, George Latimer and Lennie Felix.* (Courtesy of the B.B.C.)

As usual with "This Is Your Life" – the show is still running 25 years on – Eamonn Andrews had a few surprises up his sleeve. Humphrey Lyttelton, Britain's foremost authority on jazz, strolled on to add his praise to the others. Eamonn asked him: "What do you think of the new Nat Gonella?" Humphrey did a double-take at Nat and replied: "Is this the new Nat Gonella, he hasn't even had a respray!" There were also recorded messages from American jazz greats Louis Armstrong and Billy Kyle but the biggest surprise came when Eamonn introduced Helen Mack, Nat's vocalist from the New Georgians. Helen had been flown over specially from California where she lived, and still does, with her husband Murray Sibley. Of course, Nat's wife, Dorothy, was also brought on, and she revealed how she had won Nat's heart with the carton of new laid eggs. The show closed with Eamonn Andrews handing Nat the famous book, and inviting him to join Humphrey Lyttelton on the bandstand with the full Georgia Jazz Band. A wonderful occasion.

The name of Gonella was news again, and papers and magazines were eager to interview him and get his opinions on various subjects. Here are a few examples. Rock n' Roll? "Well, people are making a lot of money out of it so it can't be all bad." Modern Jazz? "Most of it is too sad and serious. It can be clever in its way but jazz to me means happiness." Money? "Now, there's a subject. Possibly, if I'd had a better education, I would have been more sensible with it. But I had to learn about money the hard way." Snobs? "I always put on my best Cockney accent, this usually embarrasses them and they soon go away."

Although booking dates were coming in thick and fast, Nat still managed to play the odd game of golf. He was a member of the Vaudeville Golfing Society, the showbiz club that has a limited membership. Nat has fond memories of many marvellous rounds of golf with his fellow entertainers. There was a tournament on a course near Blackpool at which he really fancied his chances of winning, and in doing so collect some of the side-bets that took place at such events. He drove off from the first tee, a wonderful shot, halfway up the fairway. His next shot was also quite magnificent, but unfortunately it rolled into a bunker. It took him fourteen strokes to get it out.

In another golf tournament at Leeds he had to play against Harry Secombe and, once again, Nat thought that he had a good chance of winning. However, just as they were about to commence the game, Harry presented Nat with a gift of twelve new golf balls. As Nat himself said: "Well, after such a generous gesture as that, I just couldn't beat him, could I?" When Nat became a victim of angina in later years, he rescinded his membership of the Vaudeville Golfing Society in order to let someone else into this elite organization. Not too many people outside the entertainment profession know that the Vaudeville Society held an annual stag-night for members, giving some of the performers a chance to let their hair down once a year, blue jokes being the order of the night. At one such gathering at the Park Lane Hotel in 1961, Nat was asked to provide a musical spot, the idea being to break up the dirty jokes. He certainly did just that; he got trumpeters Eddie Calvert and Roy Castle with the Three King Brothers to join him on the stage for a fifteen-minute jazz session that terminated with an impression of the Temperance Seven, who were going great guns at the time with "Driving Me Crazy". When they had finished, the response from the audience was tremendous, around one thousand people gave them a standing ovation.

One of Nat's most unusual television appearances in the early 1960s was when he was booked for a religious programme, "Sunday Break". One moment a group are on the screen seriously discussing religion, and the next there is Nat, blowing hot jazz. This amused him for in his early days in the music profession, ministers were always preaching that jazz was the "music of the Devil".

His come-back meant returning to the old routine, late hours and lots of travelling. Dorothy Gonella viewed the return to this way of life with mixed feelings, after all, Nat was now 54. Still, she was sensible enough to realize that this is what the entertainment profession is all about, you have to earn a crust while you can, there is no company pension waiting at the end of the road. But she still worried about him. After one Saturday night gig in Nottingham, he arrived home at five o'clock in the morning. His first words to a half-asleep Dorothy were "What a catastrophe." He took off his shoes, still muttering "What a catastrophe." By this time, Dorothy was fully awake. "What catastrophe?" she said. Nat dolefully shook his head and replied: "What Blackburn did to Spurs on Saturday."

The Georgia Jazz Band had a good run. Their drummer, the late Lennie Hastings, had happy memories of his days with Nat and the band on the road: "I left Alex Welsh on two or three occasions you know, once to join Johnny Duncan, and another time I took my own band to Germany. It was a good band but I was let down by an agent who promised me work if I came back to Britain. It was annoying for I'd gone over big in Germany and a major television company had asked me to stay out there. So, I was stuck back in Britain without anything lined up. Then an agency asked me if I was interested in making a come-back with Nat Gonella, I accepted immediately. It was great, he was marvellous to work with, very easy-going and a gentleman. I'll never forget one particular night at the 100 Club, all the young trumpet turks were up on stage, blowing their brains out, guys such as Mike Cotton, Kenny Ball and Colin Smith. Then Nat came on with his horn and absolutely showed them all the way home, playing marvellously."

In February 1961, a year after the television "This Is Your Life" show, Nat did something in a similar vein in the recording studio for Denis Preston, the end product being an L.P. titled "The Nat Gonella Story". The record contained songs that had played a prominent part in his career, and they were linked by Nat himself with associated anecdotes. The numbers included "Wild Man Blues", "Bessie Couldn't Help It", "Miss Otis Regrets", "Oh Monah", "Georgia On My Mind", "Them There Eyes", "Nagasaki", "Honeysuckle Rose", "Just A Kid Named Joe", "Ain't Misbehavin' ", "If I Only Had Wings", "Stomping At The Savoy", "Don't Get Around Much Anymore", and "Five Minutes More". Backing Nat's trumpet and vocals the record had the talents of Tony Coe, Don Lusher, Jimmy Skidmore, Stan Tracey, Phil Seamen, Lennie Bush, Roy Plummer, Sammy Stokes, Harry Smith,

*Two classic Gonella stage characteristics.* (Gonella Collection)

Ernie Shear, Stan Roderick, Jock Bain and Joe Temperly. A memorable session indeed, in fact, Philips reissued the record in 1984.

Following his success in the early Sixties, Nat's fortunes were mixed for the rest of the decade. The musical tastes of the paying public had changed yet again, bands were out, groups with twanging guitars were in. Even the dance floor had undergone a revolution, upright-style dancing with couples gliding gracefully across the ballroom was replaced by people gyrating while standing about three feet away from each other.

The Georgia Jazz Band disbanded, and Nat was once more out on his own. It was back to clubs, pubs, dinner-dances, and, eventually, a return to the variety stage. The trials and tribulations of a solo musician playing on the latter were best described by Nat himself: "Man, you just cannot imagine the kind of jam that emerges out of an orchestra pit. I couldn't stand the awful row, and I had to blow like hell to try and drown it."

His last recording date was in 1965 but he was not called upon to sing or play jazz on the record, an L.P. of the hit musical "Oliver" on the Society label. Nat played the part of Fagin, the devious Jewish receiver. Singing numbers such as "Gotta Pick a Pocket or Two".

As his work opportunities were mostly in the North of England, Nat and Dorothy moved home to the Blackpool area. In addition to his variety show appearances, he still managed to play in local jazz clubs. Nat was now in his sixties. Unlike most folk when they reach this age, with its tell-tale signs such as baggy eyes and aching backs, showbiz people have an additional burden to bear, they have to appear in shows with other veteran entertainers. Nat went on tour with "Those Were The Days" for Liverpool impresario Don Ellis, the cast included Peter Cavanagh, the impressionist, Welsh comedienne Gladys Morgan (her with the maniacal laugh), and singer Adelaide Hall.

On 7 March 1973, Nat Gonella reached the age of sixty-five. He announced his retirement from the entertainment profession, and duly reported to the local post office in Leyland, Lancashire, to collect his first week's State pension. At the time, he and Dorothy had a nice little bungalow in Leyland. Although he had abandoned the touring life, Nat still did the occasional gig in jazz clubs, usually following the arrival of a large gas or electricity bill.

At this stage in his life, it seemed likely that Nat, his trumpet, and his pile of old 78 r.p.m. records were destined to fade gracefully into the sunset. However, it was not to be. Nat received a telephone call from Ted Easton, his contact in Paris some twenty years earlier. When the American forces disbanded their bases in France, Ted drifted into Holland, formed a jazz band, and subsequently opened his own club. The object of Ted's call was to persuade Nat to go to Holland and appear at his club as a guest artiste. Ted Easton's club was in Schveningen so, no doubt prompted by his memories of forty years earlier when he had played at the Dutch resort with Ray Noble, Nat agreed to go.

He duly arrived in Holland and, after a chat about old times, Nat and Ted got down to rehearsing the guest spot. Ted happened to mention "Oh Monah", which had remained a personal favourite of Nat's since the Roy Fox days, so he included it in his act at the club. What a momentous decision it turned out to be. It was a late show and by the time his first night was over, Nat had performed "Oh Monah" no fewer than nine times. The Dutch jazz fans really took the song to their hearts, the attraction being that they could participate by singing the refrain with Nat. Word spread and the next night a recording team turned up to capture Nat performing it live with the Easton band, the intention being to add it to an L.P. They paid Ted, Ted paid Nat, and that was it – forgotten. Three years later, Nat had an urgent request to return to Holland, it seemed that "Oh Monah" had been released as a single, and had reached number five in the Dutch hit parade.

When Nat's plane touched down in Holland, he was given the kind of welcome that is usually reserved for superstars such as Frank Sinatra or Elizabeth Taylor, it was absolutely overwhelming. He was driven in an open car to meet the Mayor of Schveningen, who officially crowned him Holland's "King of Jazz". He had a medal on a red, white and blue ribbon placed over his head, and two pretty young ladies kissed him and presented him with a bouquet.

*Ted Easton arranges an airport welcome for Nat in Holland, 1977.* (Courtesy Foto Bormann)

They really gave him the star treatment. With his typical Cockney cheekiness, he inquired whether there was 20,000 guilders a year to go with the medal. Yes, it was great to see Ted and his band again, and simply wonderful to be back in Holland, a country for which Nat always had a warm affection.

Jazz has always had a strong following in Holland, as any visiting jazz celebrity could verify. American jazzmen made regular visits over the years, and while he was there, Nat had the pleasure of playing with several of them. He had memorable sessions with tenor-saxophonists Bud Freeman and Buddy Tate, trumpeter Wild Bill Davison, pianist Dick Cary, and clarinettists Peanuts Hucko and Bob Wilbur. The latter happens to be Nat's favourite clarinet player.

During his Dutch stay, Nat was entertained by a remarkable character named Fritz Van Hoff, who played the banjo in one of Ted Easton's bands. Fritz was also a wizard at mechanics and

*Nat entertains his Dutch fans, after being crowned "King of Jazz".* (Courtesy Wout Meppelink)

electronics, as Nat discovered when he stayed as a guest at his house. Nat had a bedroom on the first floor and about three o'clock in the morning he began to wish that he had not had that last drink, the call of nature being particularly strong. He crept down a spiral staircase to reach the toilet below, being careful not to wake the rest of the household. Imagine his surprise as he opened the toilet to be met by "Boing boing boing, Boing boing boing, Boing boing boing boing boing boing". Brahm's Lullaby. In the still of the night it sounded like the massed bands of the Irish Guards. It was a sample of Fritz's gadgetry. Nat did what he had to do and got out of the toilet as soon as possible but as he opened the door Brahm's boomed out again. He climbed back up the stairs before anyone appeared on the scene to see him wearing only a short vest.

However, that was not the last of Fritz's little surprises. The following morning Nat was sitting in the garden with Fritz when his host offered him a cup of coffee. Fritz produced a control panel and began operating switches and pushing buttons, then to Nat's amazement a small model train emerged from out of the garage and glided along a track that ran all the way around the garden, eventually arriving at the spot where the two men were sitting. The engine had a small truck attached to it which held two cups of coffee and a box of biscuits.

One of Nat's most memorable concerts with the Ted Easton Jazz Band was when he was accompanied at the microphone by Beryl Bryden, and we may be glad that a recording team was on hand to capture this happy occasion, with an enthusiastic audience showing their appreciation for rabble-rousing numbers such as "Bill Bailey Won't You Please Come Home?" Beryl Bryden, an ardent Gonella fan from the time he formed the Georgians, is also a gifted artist and has sketched many fine portraits of some of the great "legends" of jazz whom she has met and played with in her colourful career as a singer and exponent of the washboard.

After he had said farewell to his many friends in Holland, Nat would fly home to Dorothy and eagerly relate all the exciting happenings of his trip. Then it would be forgotten, it was back to the quiet life of retirement. On reflection, it seems strange that a jazz musician of Nat's stature should exist in comparative obscurity in his own country yet, on the Continent he was revered by millions of fans. In fact, the name of Gonella is still regarded highly in countries such as Sweden, Germany, and of course Holland. Hungary? No, it is unlikely that Hungarians still say "Harry Roy" for hello, or "Nat Gonella" for goodbye!

Retirement usually allows one to indulge more frequently in that comfortable fireside companion the armchair and as he sits in his, Nat's mind often strays back to those heady days of the past when everybody knew Nat Gonella, and it seemed that he knew everybody. There is one particular memory that stands out in his mind more than any other and it took place only in 1977. During a visit to Holland, Nat was sitting in an open square drinking coffee at a cafe when a radio disc jockey happened to play "Oh Monah", featuring Nat. A number of Dutch boys and girls were playing in the square but when the record came on they immediately stopped what they were doing in order to sing along with "Oh Monah". The effect was tremendous, deeply touching Nat, in fact, he was so choked-up he was almost in tears. The sight and sound of those little Dutch kids singing along so merrily to his song would remain with him for the rest of his life.

*Nat with Monty Sunshine, 1982.*

# 11

Although they were comfortable in their little bungalow in Lancashire, in the mid-1970s Nat had a hankering to return to where it had all begun for him, down south. Having previously lived in Southampton for many years, both Nat and Dorothy were well acquainted with the Portsmouth area, and Dorothy was born in Old Portsmouth. When she was quite young, her family moved across the harbour to neighbouring Gosport, where she went to school.

Nestling on the western shores of Portsmouth Harbour, Gosport is a pleasant town serving as a dormitory for the Royal Navy and Portsmouth Dockyard. It was in this attractive corner of Hampshire that Nat and Dorothy decided to spend the rest of their days, living in a quaint white cottage close to the beach and the main town area.

In 1978, Ken and Molly Barton, the proprietors of the Park Hotel in the Alverstoke area of Gosport, started running weekly jazz sessions on the premises. One night, someone spotted Nat in the audience and he was duly invited to sing with the resident band, which happened to be Doug and Dorry Whitfield's Riverside Jazz Band. Nat obliged with "When You're Smiling", and in response to the enthusiastic cries of "More!" he sang "Georgia On My Mind". It so happened that a showbiz columnist on a local newspaper was in the audience to do a jazz write-up. The following week the paper devoted a good deal of space to Nat Gonella's impromptu appearance. From that moment on the Park Hotel was packed with patrons every Thursday night, all hoping to see and hear the legendary Nat Gonella.

Although he no longer played the trumpet, his voice was better than ever, probably due to the fact that because he did not have to

*Still chuckling 50 years on, Nat Gonella and Tiny Winters in 1982.*

worry about playing the horn, he was able to develop his singing style and actually improve on the same songs that he had sung for so many years. A good example would be his version of "St. James Infirmary Blues", delivered with a comedy timing worthy of Max Miller. Risque? Certainly, but it is put over in such a way that it is acceptable, and blends with the earthy atmosphere of jazz. Nat Gonella and George Melly are probably two of the few performers who could get away with it.

Inspired by Nat's presence, Gosport Jazz Club went from strength to strength. Under the guidance of Pat and Tony Wing, the club moved to larger premises at Gosport Borough Football Club ground, gradually developing into a popular venue for followers of jazz in the South. Many top names have been persuaded to make the journey to Gosport, no doubt encouraged by the prospect of meeting and playing with Nat Gonella. The list includes the Pete Allen Band, Alan Elsdon, Monty Sunshine, Ken Colyer, Steve Lane, Rusty Taylor, Max Collie, Harry Gold (with his Pieces of Eight), and Digby Fairweather.

In 1983, Gosport fans had an unexpected bonus on one of Digby's visits when he brought with him ex-Georgians in the form of Tiny Winters, Pat Smuts, and Jim Shepherd. Nat singing once again with Tiny on bass, Pat on tenor sax and Jim on the trombone, plus Digby Fairweather's fine trumpet playing, produced a night of nostalgia that is unlikely to be repeated. It was all the more remarkable when one considered that the combined ages of Nat, Tiny and Pat, seventy-five, seventy-four and seventy-three respectively, totalled two hundred and twenty-two. The success of this show prompted Digby to embark on a concert tour with "A Tribute To Nat Gonella". Promoted by Jazz Services, the show included Tiny Winters and Jack Fallon, another ex-Georgian, in every concert. But, of course, it was not until the show came to Gosport that the subject of the tribute made a live appearance. Another wonderful night of music and memories.

So, the 1980s has seen a great Gonella revival, his old recordings are given a regular airing on B.B.C. radio via Alan Dell's "Dance

*Gosport Jazz Club, 1983. Tiny Winters on bass, aged 74, Nat Gonella aged 75, and Pat Smuts on tenor-sax at the age of 73.*

*Nat with clarinettist Bob Layzell and jazz veteran Harry Gold, 1984.*

Band Days" programme, and on Radio Solent, the B.B.C. station based in Southampton, on Gerry Didymus's "78 Nostalgia Show", and Chris Walker's "Solent Jazz". Jazz presenter Tim Colwell featured Nat in special tribute lasting two hours on Portsmouth's commercial station Radio Victory. Recorded at the Park Hotel, it was styled on the lines of "This Is Your Life". Also, several Nat Gonella L.P.s have been released in recent years by E.M.I., Decca, Philips and Saville, and it is inevitable that he should turn up on other records in the nostalgia vein featuring Billy Cotton, Roy Fox and Lew Stone.

How about the rest of the Gonella family? Following his spell with Nat and the Georgians after the war, Bruts Gonella made a steady living playing with several top bands, including Harry Leader and his Band, Harry Gold and his Pieces of Eight, Sid Milward and his Nitwits, among others. In the early 1960s, Bruts and his wife, Shelley, with their sons Ian and Seamus, emigrated to Australia. They enjoyed the life Down Under, and eventually settled in New South Wales. Bruts kept blowing the horn, playing with many of the top names in Australia, from the big-band format to smaller jazz groups. The two brothers had a grand reunion in recent years when Bruts and Shelley returned to visit Nat and Dorothy.

Apart from Bruts, Nat's sisters, Jessie and Lillie, are still alive out of the original seven Gonella children. Finally, we have Natalie, Nat's daughter from his first marriage. Natalie is very happily married and lives in the West Country and, although she never pursued a career in music, despite the mid-Thirties photo of her with a trumpet, she has some claim to fame as an excellent golfer. Of course, in his time Nat also swung a mean club.

One may reflect that Nat Gonella has done pretty well for a chap who was warned over sixty years ago that he would have to take things easy for the rest of his life. However, although he proved the doctors wrong, over the last decade he has had problems with what he describes as his "dodgy heart". Following a couple of spells in

*Nat singing his classic theme song* Georgia On My Mind *accompanied by Digby Fairweather on trumpet.* (Courtesy of Malcolm Macdonald)

*The "Legend of Jazz" who gave pleasure to millions, a photograph taken to celebrate Nat's 75th birthday.* (Courtesy of Malcolm Macdonald)

hospital, Nat confided that he thought that he was going to meet Gabriel, God's first trumpet. Describing one occasion in which he collapsed outside a supermarket, Nat said with a twinkle in his eye: "Yes, I had a sort of fit," adding with a gleeful chuckle, "You know, it took five men to hold me down!"

Nat gave all his friends a nasty fright in October 1984 when he had to be taken into hospital, and underwent an unpleasant operation that left him very weak. His voice was almost non-existent, and it seemed that we would never hear those distinctive Gonella vocal tones again. However, we had not reckoned on his chirpy Cockney resilience. After an absence of over two months, Nat and Dorothy made an unheralded appearance at Pat and Tony Wing's special New Year's Eve party at Gosport Jazz Club. As he entered the club, the atmosphere became electric, nearly two hundred merrymakers stopped what they were doing to turn and spontaneously applaud

*A group of famous jazz names enjoy a joke at the Nat Gonella TV show at Southsea on 1 April 1985. l to r: Beryl Bryden, Humphrey Lyttelton, Nat, Digby Fairweather and Mr Turner, former manager of the Savoy Ballroom at Southsea.*

*Nat with Humphrey Lyttelton (centre) and Digby Fairweather (left) at a concert at Southsea, Hants., arranged by the B.B.C. to celebrate the fiftieth anniversary of the Georgians' first variety tour appearance on 1 April, 1985. (Courtesy of Malcolm Macdonald)*

Nat and Dorothy as they made their way to their table. It was a most moving moment for everybody present that night was clearly so pleased to see him back. Later in the evening, before 1984 bowed out in favour of 1985, the band struck up with "When You're Smiling" and to everyone's delight Nat stood up without any prompting in order to jump on to the stage to take the microphone and provide the vocal. It was sheer magic and rather reminiscent of that moment in the "Jolson Story" when Al is called out of the nightclub audience to sing after a long absence from the stage. Although he was not quite back to his former lung power, Nat was clearly pleased and confided afterwards: "Great! Quite honestly, after the sort of operation that I had, I thought that I would be singing more like Gracie Fields."

Nat's own view on his life may be detected from a newspaper interview that he gave over twenty years ago in which he said: "If I died tomorrow, I wouldn't regret a single thing. I've had a million laughs!"

# Index

SELECT DISCOGRAPHY
(Available at time of publication)

"MISTER RHYTHM MAN" Nat Gonella & His Georgians 1934–35.
EMI Retrospect Series EG 26 0188 1
Don't Let Your Love Go Wrong; Moonglow; Troublesome Trumpet; Dinah; Let Him Live; Oh Mo'nah; Georgia On My Mind; Sing, It's Good For Ya; E Flat Blues; Georgia's Gorgeous Gal; Basin Street Blues; I'm Gonna Wash My Hands Of You; Mister Rhythm Man; Stardust; An Earful Of Music; Down T'Uncle Bill's; Smoke Rings; Beale Street Blues; Rockin' Chair; I Heard; St. Louis Blues; Runnin' Wild; Rhythm Is Our Business; Breakin' The Ice.

"NAT GONELLA – GEORGIA ON MY MIND".
Decca Recollections Series RFL 12
At The Woodchopper's Ball; There's A Cabin In The Pines; Georgia On My Mind; You've Got Me Crying Again; I Can't Dance, I Got Ants In My Pants; Stardust; Nagasaki; Rolling In The Hay; Murder; For No Reason At All; Sweet Sixteen And Never Been Kissed; Isle Of Capri; Fit As A Fiddle; Gnat Jump; I Haven't Time To Be A Millionaire; So Shy; Oh Mo'nah; Miss Otis Regrets.

"THE NAT GONELLA STORY".
Philips-British Traditional Jazz Series. Stereo 6459 218
Georgia; Wild Man Blues; Bessie Couldn't Help it; Miss Otis Regrets; Them There Eyes; Oh Mo'nah; If I Only Had Wings; Nagasaki; Honeysuckle Rose; Just A Kid Named Joe; Ain't Misbe-

170

havin';Stompin' At The Savoy; Don't Get Around Much Any More; Five Minutes More.

'THE GOLDEN AGE OF NAT GONELLA'
Music For Pleasure Series. GX 4125361
Nagasaki; I'm Confessin' That I Love You; The Japanese Sandman; Fascinating Rhythm; Blue, Turning Grey Over You; Hesitation Blues; The Toy Trumpet; The Skeleton In The Cupboard; Ain't Misbehavin'; Singin' The Blues; I Can't Dance, I Got Ants In My Pants; Truckin'; Caravan; I'm Nobody's Baby; Can't Get Indiana Off My Mind; The Sheik Of Araby.